BECOMING AMERICANS

BECOMING AMERICANS:
OUR STRUGGLE TO BE BOTH FREE AND EQUAL

A Plan of Thematic Interpretation

Cary Carson, Editor

The Colonial Williamsburg Foundation
Williamsburg, Virginia

Library of Congress Cataloging-in-Publication Data

Becoming Americans : our struggle to be both free and equal : a plan
of thematic interpretation / Cary Carson, editor.
  p. cm.
  Includes bibliographical references.
  ISBN 0-87935-167-5
  1. Williamsburg (Va.)—History—Study and teaching. 2. Historic
sites—Interpretive programs—Virginia—Williamsburg. 3. Curriculum
planning—Virginia—Williamsburg. 4. Public history—Virginia—
Williamsburg. I. Carson, Cary.
F234.W7B43 1998
975.5'4252—dc21   98-10785
                           CIP

Designed by Helen M. Olds

Photography by David M. Doody, Tom Green, Hans Lorenz, and
other Colonial Williamsburg staff photographers

Printed in China

CONTENTS

The Williamsburg story, which we call
"Becoming Americans," tells how diverse peoples,
holding different and sometimes conflicting personal
ambitions, evolved into a society that valued both liberty
and equality. Americans cherish these values as their
birthright, even when their promise remains unfulfilled.

Interpretation at Colonial Williamsburg
explores the history behind critical challenges that
currently divide American society and the historic forces
that simultaneously unite it.

PREFACE

This published edition of Colonial Williamsburg's newest educational plan comes on the heels of five preliminary drafts that circulated to staff members and outside readers since the first was issued in January 1994. Each subsequent draft has incorporated comments and suggestions from interpreters, teachers, historians, curators, officers, and trustees—and now from copyeditors as well.

While the process of consultation and revision, which stretched out over three years, may at times have seemed laborious and protracted, each draft has improved on the last. The story lines have grown stronger. The "Becoming Americans" theme has become more tightly woven into the historical narrative. Little by little, the entire plan has assumed the shape of interpretation at Colonial Williamsburg. It begins to look like a new suit of clothes after the third or fourth fitting.

It should. Rewriting *Teaching History at Colonial Williamsburg* has been a thoroughly collaborative undertaking from the beginning. Thirty work groups discussed the first draft and submitted comments to the authors. Interpreters and staff historians took part in a pilot program four summers ago to test experimental story lines at several exhibition buildings and trade shops in the Historic Area. The following spring, more than sixty self-nominated interpreters, historians, and curators reexamined and completely rewrote the historical story lines that this plan now presents in final form. Never before in Colonial Williamsburg's seventy-year history have so many educators throughout the foundation pooled their talents to create a comprehensive plan of interpretation.

For whom is this book intended? For our own interpreters, curators, and historians first and foremost. By now we know that there will be other readers too. Numerous requests from schoolteachers sent the previous plan into extra printings. Sometimes even visitors have asked for something that they can take home to continue learning the history lessons they encountered first on the streets of Williamsburg. The latest revised edition of *Teaching History* therefore includes topical discussions and recommended readings for outside audiences as well as for staff.

Acknowledgments

We—the four undersigned authors of the first draft of this new educational plan—have accumulated debts of gratitude in ever-growing numbers as one draft after another brought more and more colleagues into collaboration. The four of us began meeting to discuss the ideas and to draft the educational plan presented in this document during the summer of 1993 as part of a comprehensive self-study project called History Initiatives. Three other teams addressed the preparation and orientation of guests, the physical appearance of the Historic Area, and the visitor's learning experience at Colonial Williamsburg. Our little group consulted frequently with the leaders of those teams, Larry Henry, John Sands, and Conny Graft. Larry and Conny read and commented on early drafts. So did Graham Hood, who led the History Initiatives study, and Steve Elliott, who later appointed and now chairs the steering group that directs the complicated task of moving ideas off these pages and onto the streets of restored Williamsburg.

We also extend thanks to our associates at the Omohundro Institute of Early American History and Culture. They reviewed the manuscript twice. On another occasion, most members of the Board of Trustees at Colonial Williamsburg attended an all-day retreat to talk about the "Becoming Americans" theme and its presentation at the museum they look after with great diligence and devotion. We are grateful, too, for Bob Wilburn's lively interest in the institution's educational mission and also for the time the vice presidents have spent discussing the plan in draft and encouraging us to proceed.

Our debts multiplied tenfold when Steve Elliott appointed several teams to rewrite the story lines. His decision shifted the burden of planning from four sets of shoulders to more than sixty. The names of all participants on those teams appear at the conclusion of each story line chapter. We thank each and every one of them, but here have space to mention only the team leaders by name—John Caramia, Christy Matthews and later Anne Willis, Pam Pettengell, Anne Schone, John Turner, and Bill White—and the historians who helped with much of the writing—Pat Gibbs, George Hassell, Cathy Hellier, Kevin Kelly, Emma L. Powers, Julie Richter, Linda Rowe, and Lorena Walsh.

Everyone's interest and advice has been welcome. We have heeded as much of it as was possible. No statement of the foundation's educational mission could amalgamate all the suggestions we were offered. Our job was to identify points of view on which there appeared to be broad agreement among our colleagues in the education, research, and collections divisions. We then looked for corresponding ideas in the most recent and relevant historical literature. From those two sources, we put into our own words—and those words into this book—a story about nation making by the remarkably diverse people who settled Virginia when Williamsburg was its capital.

CARY CARSON
KEVIN KELLY
CHRISTY MATTHEWS
BILL WHITE

At the Raleigh Tavern, visitors eavesdrop on character interpreters arguing about the nonimportation of British goods.

THE "BECOMING AMERICANS" THEME

Picture-perfect Williamsburg! A beguiling half-truth that invites time travelers
to discover the rest of the story around the corner.

THE "BECOMING AMERICANS" THEME

For many Americans, Colonial Williamsburg needs no introduction. Millions have heard the often-told story of John D. Rockefeller, Jr.'s, restoration of Virginia's eighteenth-century capital. Millions more have strolled down its picture-book streets and admired its restored and reconstructed buildings standing behind neat picket fences. Visitors return again and again to sample its great collection of English and American decorative arts. They marvel at the handiwork of ingenious artisans who practice mysteries long thought forgotten. They discover their own roots in stories about ordinary people and everyday life skillfully told by knowledgeable interpreters. They take inspiration from the fact that George Washington, Thomas Jefferson, James Madison, George Mason, and Patrick Henry debated fundamental concepts of American democracy in this provincial capital on the edge of England's empire. So indelibly is "America's Williamsburg" inked into the mythology of our national heritage that those of us whom the foundation employs as educators are often hard pressed to help visitors see beyond Williamsburg's picture-postcard reputation and to appreciate the substantive historical issues that can make their encounter with the past deep and enduring.

Appearances are deceiving. Colonial Williamsburg is more than meets the eye. Repeat visitors have learned to expect the unexpected. While many admired landmarks on this restored and reconstructed townscape endure from one generation to another, our historical interpretations are continuously revised and reinvented. No end of programs explore new ways to help visitors think for themselves about meanings, ideas, and relationships, past and present. Our commitment to innovation, experimentation, and self-improvement runs deep—sometimes all the way back to first principles. Periodically, the foundation's educators overhaul the museum's educational plan to correct past mistakes, to set interpretation in a new direction, and to teach history better. The following revised, expanded, and entirely rewritten edition of the Colonial Williamsburg plan is our latest attempt to surprise people's expectations, no matter how well they know us or how often they return.

LESSON PLANNING

To teach history effectively, program planners at Colonial Williamsburg know that we must successfully juggle four elements in the learning process. Most important are the personal interests of visitors and their concerns about contemporary life. Those priorities shape—or sometimes misshape—their understanding of the past. Next are the historical themes and topics that we museum historians and interpreters select to tell the Williamsburg story in ways that give visitors a perspective on themselves and on American society. A third element is the special teaching techniques that interpreters use to help visitors visualize and imagine a world that vanished two hundred years ago. Finally, there is the celebrated collection of original buildings and antique furnishings that people come to see—the restored and refurnished eighteenth-century town that makes the history lessons seem real to the history learners. All four must work together before interpretation can speak loudly and clearly to the visiting public.

Every few years, the questions that thoughtful citizens continually ask about themselves, their society, and the world around them require a fresh perspective. A museum must adjust its plan of education accordingly. That time has come again at Colonial Williamsburg.

The 1985 edition of *Teaching History* challenged us to broaden our interpretation of the past to include the many eighteenth-century residents of the town whose lives and contributions had been insufficiently acknowledged in earlier tellings. That important work is well started, but it remains far from finished. So we renew our commitment to teach a history of early Virginia that describes and celebrates the diverse backgrounds of Indians, slaves, and settlers. Yet, even as we hasten to piece together this cultural mosaic, we recognize that it, too, must keep step with the contemporary concerns that our visitors bring to their museum experience. Remarkable events, here and abroad, have started people thinking anew about the common life that citizens share with one another despite their many differences.

Americans who read books about history, watch it on television, and visit history museums are mindful as never before of their diverse origins, resilient ethnic and cultural traditions, and long history of unequal treatment and contentious relations. At the same time, growing numbers of men and women are coming to realize that they also believe—or want to believe—that "We the People" represents a shared experience that is greater than the sum of the nation's many parts. In the search for a more coherent national narrative, including the part that Colonial Williamsburg can tell, we cannot minimize minority rights, smooth over the reality of social conflict in American history, or de-emphasize the country's extraordinary patchwork of unassimilated ethnic cultures and customs. Thanks to social historians, we have learned too much about ourselves to accept the oversimplified fiction implied by the motto

Programs at Colonial Williamsburg draw a cross section of visitors who closely resemble the educated, middle-class, ethnically mixed urban population that makes up most museum audiences. African-Americans account for 2 to 5 percent of visitors.

E pluribus unum. Thanks, too, to recent work by political historians, we know that the principles of democratic republicanism on which our system of government was founded embody unreconciled and irreconcilable contradictions and tensions between the rights guaranteed to self-interested individuals and the common good promised to all who join together in a state of society.

Informed citizens openly acknowledge the differences that divide us and the inconsistencies in our governing philosophy. Now more than ever, history learners anxiously seek historical precedents to bolster their hope that greater social diversity need not end in the disintegration of American institutions. They look to the past for guidance at a time when ethnic and racial hatreds are tearing apart settled societies around the globe and poisoning living communities closer to home.

Visitors bring these feelings of uncertainty to their learning experience at Colonial Williamsburg. Their recognition of and pride in the diversity of American society is complicated by a growing concern that American culture is falling to pieces. Their anxiety is a state of mind to which museum historians and interpreters should respond. As teachers of popular history, we are important agents of change. We show thoughtful men and women how Americans have always been engaged in reinventing the nation and redefining the qualifications for citizenship.

The War for Independence from Great Britain and the adoption of a federal Constitution and Bill of Rights did not lay the great nation-making issues to rest once and for all. Far from it. The bonds they loosed and the contradictions they papered over led rapidly to a state of affairs that sounds astonishingly current to today's museum visitors. From the moment of its birth, the United States appeared ready to disintegrate into a thousand selfish interests. The "tender connection among men" that the Revolution was supposed to foster, one observer said, was "reduced to nothing [by] the infinite diversities of family, tribe, and nation." A foreign traveler to the newly independent country discovered, to his surprise and dismay, a "world . . . unfortunately composed . . . of discordant atoms, jumbled together by chance, and tossed by inconstancy in an immense vacuum." Founding father John Adams, writing years later to another, Thomas Jefferson, bewailed the course of events that the two of them had set in motion: "Where is now, the progress of the human Mind? . . . When? Where? and how? is the present Chaos to be arranged into Order?" The forces of individualism and radical egalitarianism unleashed by the Revolution and the equally powerful forces of order and containment have been vying with one another at the heart of America for two hundred years. Long before that, those forces were gathering strength and direction throughout the period we interpret at Colonial Williamsburg.

History is never a handbook of ready-made answers to the critical choices that divide modern American society, however close the parallels may sometimes appear. Nevertheless, history learners can and should take encouragement from the knowledge that our traditions and values have deep roots, even the divisive ones. They need to know that our institutions have stood the test of time. Little by little, and often slowly and reluctantly, those who control those institutions have yielded to irresistible pressures to share the country's opportunities more widely and to include an ever-broader segment of the population in the civic enterprise. The narrative of this continuing struggle to expand or to limit the universal citizenship promised by the Declaration of Independence is the dynamic plot running through the story that we have taken for our central theme and call "Becoming Americans."

That phrase appeared first in a report written in 1977 by a group calling itself the Curriculum Committee. It reappeared eight years later in the earliest published edition of *Teaching History at Colonial Williamsburg*. Initially, it was explained as a process of cultural transformation, as a story of two immigrant peoples—one African, the other European—who met in a land unfamiliar to both. Over the course of several generations, they developed distinctively different, yet distinctively American, white and black cultures.

We still believe that "Becoming Americans" is a story worth telling at Colonial Williamsburg. But how should it be brought up to date with recent scholarship? What have we learned from the experience of interpreters who have presented the theme publicly for over a decade? Most of all, how should a new educational plan respond to the concerns and questions that visitors will bring to their museum learning experience at the end of the twentieth century and beyond?

The cast of African and European historical characters who were featured in a "Becoming Americans" story set in eighteenth-century Virginia corresponded twenty years ago to the two audiences we were most eager to engage in a dialogue about race relations—African-Americans and whites. Since then, the national discourse on race and ethnicity has expanded and grown more complex with the arrival of more than twenty-three million immigrants since 1970, most of them from Asia and Latin America. Native Americans' contributions to American history and identity also deserve reappraisal and appreciation. Gender issues have added women's voices to the debate as well.

The task of revising the plan becomes harder still if we consider the astonishing and unexpected recent events in Russia, the former Soviet republics, and uprooted nations around the world that have called renewed attention to America's immigrant experience and its experiment in secular democratic capitalism. These are some of the new issues and audiences to which our educational programs must respond by redefining what the "Becoming Americans" theme will mean to us and our visitors in the years ahead.

Residents of Williamsburg in the eighteenth century were mostly newcomers from Great Britain or West Africa or their offspring. Today, "Becoming Americans" tells their stories in ways that recent immigrants and new Americans from everywhere recognize as their stories too.

An estate sale that included four chattel slaves was reenacted on the steps of Wetherburn's Tavern in October 1994. It drew a crowd of two thousand spectators and received network television coverage.

AMERICAN HISTORY IN MINIATURE

Long ago, Colonial Williamsburg taught the history of colonial Virginia as if it were the opening chapter to American history generally. Today, we recognize that such presumption fails to do justice to the ancestry of Native American cultures and to the earlier settlements on these shores by England's colonial rivals, Spain and France. While leaving such exaggerated claims behind, our new "Becoming Americans" plan aspires to an educational goal hardly less ambitious than its predecessor. Our outdoor classroom may only be the size of a small southern town, and the period of time we interpret may barely cover the hundred years when Williamsburg was the seat of provincial government. Yet, these limitations need not restrict the intellectual dimensions of the ideas and issues that we use this restored capital city to present. The first edition of *Teaching History* encouraged interpreters to help visitors think about race and culture in the broadest terms imaginable. This second edition expands the "Becoming Americans" theme in still other directions because questions of race and culture have since become complicated by problems of citizenship and nationhood.

How do we tell a Williamsburg-size story so that it looks and sounds like a history of nation building? To put the question another way, how do we focus interpretation on the political and economic struggle to expand popular participation in civic culture without letting the separate stories of ordinary people—the social histories that many interpreters have learned to present so well—drift off to the edges of historical consciousness? Recent scholarship in American history is working on a solution to the second problem: how to make connections between people's private lives and their public culture. Interpreters' mastery of the art of social history storytelling suggests an answer to the first: how to tell a big story on the streets of a small town.

American historians—a little ahead of their audiences—have come to appreciate that the distinctive values and beliefs that give this nation its identity have been formed in a complex, never-ending, give-and-take process of conflict and accommodation. At stake always have been the aspirations of ordinary people. The philosophical and constitutional principles that validated those aspirations came later. The matters most fundamentally at issue have been the most commonplace things in people's lives—their work, their wealth, their reputations, their family and friends, their health and creature comforts, the salvation of their souls, and all the other pressing realities of daily living. Problems arose when one person's or one group's hopes and fears conflicted with those of others. Shared values and accepted norms were arrived at only by confrontation, negotiation, and accommodation (or sometimes were settled swiftly by coercion) between individuals and groups who began with different and conflicting interests.

This ceaseless tug-of-war among self-interested parties is the central

Boy Scouts learn that apprentices worked for more than merit badges in Hay's Cabinetmaking Shop.

dynamic in our democracy. It has always been the aggressive force that challenged the status quo and undermined the prevailing balance of power. Because historians try to explain why things changed in the past to get us ready to understand and deal with changes still to come, history teachers and history learners pay close attention to conflicts and the ways they were (or were not) resolved. "Becoming Americans" is a dynamic story in that narrative tradition. Its emphasis on conflict over concord should not be taken to imply that we believe that all was chaos and disorder in eighteenth-century America. The clash of interests deserves our special attention mainly because those were the encounters that profoundly reshaped American identities and American values.

Private lives, historians are rediscovering, are always lived in and through institutions larger than the family. Some, such as churches and law courts, are formal organizations. Other institutions are merely patterns of expected actions enforced by social sanctions—folk customs, rules of etiquette, and "gentlemen's agreements," for example. Public and private are not autonomous spheres, as we often mistakenly believe. Social history and civic history are inextricably united. The "Becoming Americans" theme recognizes that in real life there are workaday connections between people's personal ambitions, the philosophies and rhetoric that they adopt to idealize and legitimate them, and the formal and informal institutions that they use to arbitrate contending values and enforce the will of those in authority. Interpretation at Colonial Williamsburg thus joins the separate strands of social history, the history of ideas, and a dynamic account of Virginia's early institutions into one unified narrative. The political story includes a fresh retelling of the events that ended with the War of Independence from Great Britain and began the real American Revolution, which transformed the new republic in so many radical and unexpected ways.

Our tours and interpretations at Colonial Williamsburg must find ways to present this larger story of the nation's past in a miniature version appropriate to the restored streetscapes and furnished buildings of the eighteenth-century town that serves as our classroom. The miniaturists are the museum's interpreters. They are accomplished in the art of teaching history by telling personal stories about men and women who lived and worked in Williamsburg. To help them select characters and story lines that illustrate the sweep of historical forces that we want visitors to understand, this new edition of the master plan provides a framework of ideas—an argument in outline—that explains, point by point, what the "Becoming Americans" theme means. The narrative outline is broadly conceived, and deliberately so, because it must shape everything we say about the colonial capital of Virginia into the one comprehensible Williamsburg story that we hope every visitor will learn. The story tells how diverse peoples, holding different and sometimes conflicting personal ambitions, evolved into a society that valued both liberty and equality. Subsequent generations of Americans have come to cherish these values as their birthright, even when the promise has remained unfulfilled. Ultimately, interpretation at Colonial Williamsburg explores the history behind the critical challenges that presently divide American society and the historic forces that simultaneously unite it.

Real-life soap operas put community standards and values on public view at county courthouses in the eighteenth century and again today in Williamsburg.

A Framework for
Explaining Change

The central theme running through all our educational programs at Colonial Williamsburg, the story we call "Becoming Americans" and subtitle "Our Struggle to Be Both Free and Equal," takes a long view of the colonial period. Its main ideas can be set out one by one. They have headings that readers will find useful when comparing the story lines presented later.

Diverse Peoples

Many different peoples met in North America in the seventeenth and eighteenth centuries—Europeans from numerous nations and regions, Africans from distant and often dissimilar societies, and Native Americans from many tribal backgrounds.

Clashing Interests

The customs, values, and beliefs that new arrivals brought to their encounters with each other and with the environment bore some superficial similarities, but more often were marked by profound differences. The experience of immigration and resettlement exaggerated differences between self-interested individuals and dissimilar ethnic and cultural groups.

Shared Values

Whether the encounters between newcomers were peaceful or confrontational, they gradually produced informal accommodations to a new set of beliefs and values that could already be discerned by the middle of the eighteenth century.

Some of these shared assumptions have become fundamental rights that all Americans expect, however diverse their backgrounds and however differently they understand and apply the following ideals:

- This country is a place where a person is free to improve his or her circumstances.

- Every citizen is entitled to pursue a private vision of personal happiness.

- Life and individual liberty are essential to that pursuit.

- These expectations are tempered by one more, equality, which Americans understand to be every person's equal worth with rights to equal justice, equal opportunities, and equal access to the civic enterprise.

- Everyone has a right and a duty to participate in the governing of society.

These values gave meaning to people's personal lives most importantly—to their family and social relationships, to their attitudes about gender, class, and race, to their work, to their ambitions for property and wealth, to their ideas and philosophies, and to their religious convictions.

FORMATIVE INSTITUTIONS

These personal values also formed the basic assumptions that created and shaped the economic, political, and cultural institutions that brought order and control to public interactions between different peoples.

Because these personal and institutional values had many practical applications in people's everyday social relations, they became defining qualities in an emerging American identity. Some served to justify the war for national independence.

PARTIAL FREEDOMS

The revolutionary debate gave voice to these principles, but later events left their great promise unfulfilled for many. Continuing inequalities of wealth, patriarchal presumptions, and antidemocratic institutions blunted the radical social implications of the revolutionary philosophy and restricted its immediate blessings to a select and privileged few.

The cultural encounters of the seventeenth and eighteenth centuries also produced the ideas and practices that resisted the egalitarian impulse. Racism, violence, environmental degradation, the exploitation of labor, and the deprecation of women became the darker side of the American experience.

REVOLUTIONARY PROMISE

Although these obstacles to the pursuit of happiness persist, the most positive and progressive American ideals have always exerted a powerful hold on the popular imagination. In spite of the inherent contradictions in these ideals and the conflicts they encourage between divergent visions of the good life, they have never ceased to raise expectations and inspire hope that more Americans may secure a meaningful voice in taking responsibility for their own lives.

To prepare this interpretive framework for presentation at Colonial Williamsburg, the outline has to be filled in with the people, places, and events of Virginia history (for a demonstration, see Appendix A). Interpreters and staff historians have begun to make those additions by populating the story lines with local historical figures and locating those interpretations in the places of exhibition that we show to visitors. Tailoring the story to Williamsburg also gives special prominence to those seminal events when the affairs of the colony and the town truly became the affairs of a nation in the making—Patrick Henry's 1765 "Caesar-Brutus" speech, the Resolution for Independence, which led directly to the July Fourth Declaration in Philadelphia, and the introduction of Thomas Jefferson's Statute for Religious Freedom. These episodes in the birth of the country happened here and nowhere else.

The choice of a comprehensive organizing theme has implications for everything we do. It helps educational planners write coherent story lines, set priorities, and select sites and programs that make efficient use of our limited resources. It gives fund-raisers a packaged program to present to donors. A theme helps individual interpreters choose what to say and show and what to

leave out. It reminds them that they have a double duty to visitors to *describe* life in the past and to *explain* how and why it came to be that way.

A common theme also gives direction to research. It sets the agenda of questions to be asked and steers historians toward the appropriate sources and methods to answer them. Choosing sites to excavate, collections to acquire and exhibit, and field and documentary studies to conduct becomes an exciting collaboration when researchers follow the same scholarly compass.

Best of all, visitors are the ultimate beneficiaries of thematic interpretations. Not only are they treated to the richly visual setting of the restored town, but its significance—its meaning—is also made plain. The past becomes intelligible, and thereby it becomes usable in the one world that visitors know best—their own.

Daily events at Colonial Williamsburg re-create tense moments in the colony's standoff with Britain. Here, visitors participate in the mock trial and execution of an effigy of the hated British Prime Minister, Lord North.

Character interpreters, coached by historians, give visitors a glimpse into people's private thoughts and deepest feelings.

A Townspeople's Story

To select a theme is to choose among many possible historical messages. Themes also influence the selection of interpretive techniques and the physical organization of the visitor's learning experience. The dynamics of our "Becoming Americans" story about the pursuit of individual happiness, the inevitable conflicts that arose, and the forging of American values in the resolution of those conflicts will require innovations in the way we present Colonial Williamsburg to the public.

Interpretation that combines social, intellectual, and institutional history into a unified narrative proceeds from the conviction that people's beliefs and actions have now—and always have had—consequences. A story about human agency is most effectively told about real men and women. Interpreters have the task of putting modern visitors into the shoes, the lives, and the stories of the Williamsburg townspeople who made the history we teach. That means finding ways to translate underlying historical forces, long-term trends, abstract ideas, developing technologies, changing fashions and styles, and other historical abstractions into the real-life hopes and fears of the men, women, and children who populate our portrayal of the eighteenth-century town we interpret to the public. Experience has taught us that museum visitors learn history best when they are invited to enter into the day-to-day circumstances of real people from the past.

A father's affections are easier demonstrated than described.

Our chosen theme further implies that townspeople and travelers to eighteenth-century Williamsburg led interconnected lives. To them, the capital city was much more than a cluster of public and private buildings organized into a gridiron of streets and alleys. The town's physical layout gave shape to a complicated network of social and occupational relationships that people formed and reformed in the course of their daily lives. Modern-day visitors frequently fail to understand that the town was once a working community. Until recently, its administrative subdivision into separately ticketed exhibition buildings and trade shops contributed to the impression that the Historic Area was the world's largest collection of side-by-side historic house museums and not a re-creation of living neighborhoods. The current system of clustering exhibit buildings and trade shops into neighborhoods is intended to encourage everybody to see the town as a whole. Interpretation that introduces visitors to people they can really meet or easily imagine takes one more step toward re-creating the personal links that formed the connective tissue of the colonial community we invite visitors to compare with their own.

That comparison will be easier to make if we act on another implication of the "Becoming Americans" theme, an idea suggested by the subtitle "Our Struggle to be Both Free and Equal." Communities in the eighteenth century were no more likely to be harmonious than they are today. Lives that were tightly intertwined frequently unraveled into disagreements and frayed into conflicts that only the law, peer pressure, or raw force could resolve. The thesis running through our central theme argues that the community's values and beliefs were formed in a collision of interests—sometimes personal ambitions, sometimes cultural differences—from which there often arose a mutually acceptable or temporarily tolerable solution. By exploring these conflicts and their resolutions, we can show visitors the generating force in the nation-making process. Not all differences erupted into open conflict. Many were patiently and silently suffered by women, children, slaves, non-Christians, and men without property, all of whom found themselves permanently disadvantaged in a society that was ruled by a class of wealthy, powerful, and privileged men. Acknowledging the fundamental inequality that underlay the eighteenth-century social order becomes the visitor's starting point in understanding the inherent imbalance of power between the haves and have-nots which drove the events that give the "Becoming Americans" story its dramatic energy.

Visitors will discover the social history background to our story in those many intimate places where the town's inhabitants lived out their lives. The story only starts there. Our new narrative also requires that we portray the townspeople of Williamsburg in the public realm where their lives connected with others outside the family and outside the workplace and where disputes among them often became matters of public concern. In the previous edition of this plan, every place of exhibition was assigned to one of four categories,

Restored stores along Duke of Gloucester Street display imported goods for sale in the front room. The storekeeper's counting room and residence are behind.

government, economy, family, or cultural life. Those subdivisions disappear with this revision. The new plan of interpretation makes a distinction only between private and public, that is, between the domestic settings and workplaces where visitors will make the acquaintance of individual men and women whose personal circumstances begin each story line and the larger civic arena where the life of the community took place.

This private/public designation need not be rigidly or categorically applied. Many buildings and outside spaces throughout the town served both purposes in the colonial period. For example, the jail and the Governor's Palace doubled as public buildings and private residences. So did taverns and sometimes stores. Many dwellings reserved public entertaining rooms for company and private chambers for members of the family and the household. Even such a thoroughly civic building as the county courthouse was a place where the personal behavior of plaintiffs and defendants was openly described, examined, and made a matter of public record. By not assigning exhibition buildings and trade shops to any one fixed category, we give ourselves the flexibility to organize our interpretations of the town at whatever locations best suit the stories we want to tell. Most often, these private and public sites are most easily understood when grouped into neighborhoods. Other times, we will want to string them together to accommodate special tours. Occasionally, an entire story line can be presented in both its public and private aspects inside the four walls of a single building or within the compass of a single outside space.

This revised educational plan gives us freedoms and responsibilities we lacked before. On one hand, our storytellers are now at liberty to treat the town as a comprehensible whole and may take their pick of the full cast of characters from the period we interpret. On the other, such license comes with the obligation to create carefully crafted interpretations that help visitors understand the history lessons we believe are most worth learning.

WRITING STORY LINES

Museum planners are not fortune tellers. They have no extraordinary powers to predict with certainty the challenges an institution will face in the future. A planning document can only give general direction to a course of study, propose an organizing theme, relate that theme to the institution's stated mission, and establish guidelines for its use in creating new programs. Beyond that, planners have to place their trust in those who will carry out the plan and apply its basic principles to needs and opportunities as they arise.

If visitors to Colonial Williamsburg have come to expect the unexpected, our long-range plans must leave our imaginations free to create future interpretations that draw on new scholarship, test innovative methods of instruction, and respond to visitors' changing interests. We achieve that versatility by recognizing that all educators at Colonial Williamsburg share responsibility for deciding how best to present our chosen theme.

The preparation of this interpretive plan lays the groundwork. It reaffirms our commitment to explore the forces that have simultaneously divided and united the nation. It gives that historical narrative a name— "Becoming Americans"—and defines it as the story of our unending endeavor to resolve the paradox between personal liberty and the pursuit of individual happiness and the equally potent ideals of social justice and opportunity for all. The plan grounds that theme in the narrative of early American history and the history of colonial Virginia (see Appendix A). It even ordains that its presentation will acquaint visitors with the personal stories of the many different men and women who lived in eighteenth-century Williamsburg and will show how their private lives were played out in the formal and informal public institutions that shaped the community's civic and social culture.

These directives take the planning process this far, but not to the next step, to the selection of story lines. That choice belongs to us all. The six story lines described in the following chapters were chosen after much discussion throughout the foundation. They have been refined and rewritten by teams

Louis Craig, an unlicensed itinerant Baptist preacher, rails against the established church before a crowd of visitors on a thematic walking tour.

Kids pitch in to help a storekeeper's slave load provisions on a freight wagon westward bound for the valley of Virginia.

of interpreters, historians, and curators. We should expect to repeat this exercise periodically during the years that this plan remains in force. Inventing new narratives to help visitors understand the evolution of American society will renew our creativity and give full play to our inventiveness.

The transformation of Virginia society can be told many different ways. Visitors have too little time to hear them all. It is therefore up to us, the foundation's scholars, educators, and marketers, to agree on a manageable number of scenarios that present the "Becoming Americans" thesis in terms that connect critical issues of the eighteenth century to some that still concern visitors today. The dramatic tension between individual rights and the common good, between liberty and equality, can animate many topics that are appropriately interpreted at Williamsburg. Some figure in our programs already—the paradox of slavery, the subordination of women, the rise of the modern family, the separation of church and state, the democratization of taste, the development of American law, and, of course, the rebellion and civil war against the tyranny of British misrule. The list of topics could be doubled or tripled. There is no dearth of histories we *might* teach.

Our challenge as public historians is to present a selection of topical narratives that offers visitors a variety of interesting, entertaining, and instructive approaches to learning our central history lesson. The six story lines described below will be phased into the interpretation of the Historic Area and Carter's Grove over a period of six years. As long as each is conceived as a fresh retelling of the larger "Becoming Americans" story, our educational program will be enriched and the central message reinforced.

To achieve consistency and to ensure that every story line explores the development of basic American values, future program planners are encouraged to write treatments that follow the framework of ideas presented on pages 12–13. The main points in that outline can be rephrased as a set of questions intended to help future story line creators develop a narrative structure that supports the central "Becoming Americans" theme. The questions have their beginning in the local Williamsburg story, but they require answers that raise the larger issues that lie at the heart of our revised plan.

1. Who are the protagonists in this story line, and what values, customs, and assumptions did they bring to their experience in Williamsburg and Virginia? [Diverse Peoples]

2. How did people's different backgrounds, ideas, and aspirations provoke conflicts, and how were their customary values and practices challenged by the unfamiliar conditions they encountered in the colonies? [Clashing Interests]

3. What accommodations were reached that most parties were prepared, resigned, or forced to live with, and how may some of these have evolved into new values, however loosely shared? [Shared Values]

4. How were these concessions institutionalized? [Formative Institutions]

5. How did those institutions favor some and disadvantage others? [Partial Freedoms]

6. In what respects did persistent injustices, inequalities, and unbalanced power relationships contain seeds of future unrest? [Revolutionary Promise]

Readers are invited to examine the story lines described in the next six chapters. Each contains answers to these questions. Each interprets an important transformation in the lives of eighteenth-century Virginians and in the development of Virginia institutions: the expropriation of the western frontier, the growth of slavery, the spread of store-bought culture, the redefinition of family relationships, the developing political and constitutional crisis with Great Britain, and the separation of church and state.

While not everyone will agree that these are the six most noteworthy episodes in Virginia history, they were chosen very deliberately. We believe that they illustrate six representative issues, each of which brings historical perspective to values and attitudes that still provoke controversy in American society. They give proof that six very different historical subjects can be organized intellectually to contribute to one coherent program of interpretation.

Workers going to the fields.

TAKING POSSESSION

Virginia, by Captain John Smith, engraving, London, 1612. John Smith's map was based on his explorations in the Chesapeake region in 1607 and 1608. Europeans' knowledge of the New World was limited to the coastline. Information about the interior came from the Indians.

TAKING POSSESSION

The "Taking Possession" story line examines the colonists' quest for land ownership and discusses how their quest affected Native Americans, settlers from other nations, and the development of fundamental American values.

KEY POINTS

- BACKGROUND AND THESIS. The availability of land fueled the immigration of Europeans to Virginia and the colony's westward expansion onto lands occupied by Native Americans.

- CROSS-CULTURAL INTERACTION. Native Americans, Europeans, and Africans attempted to secure their own interests—which differed according to their cultural values—through trade, negotiation, and armed conflict. None emerged unscathed or unchanged.

- LAND ACQUISITION. The colonists' exploration, mapping, acquisition, and exploitation of land evolved from European cultural and legal precedents and consumed much of their time and resources.

- WILLIAMSBURG'S CENTRAL ROLE. As the capital of a vast territory, Williamsburg was the center of shifting networks of political, economic, diplomatic, and military relationships that linked colonial Virginians, European powers, Native American groups, and other colonies.

- WILLIAMSBURG AS A HUB. It was a commercial, administrative, and communications center and home to many institutions and activities— the passage of laws, the licensing of surveyors, the recording of transactions, and the negotiation and adjudication of disputes—that shaped Virginians' relationships to the land.

- LEGACY. In the process of taking possession of the land for themselves, colonial Virginians altered the environment and began to develop an exploitative land-use ideology.

- LAND OWNERSHIP. The emergence of a large freeholding population fostered Americans' belief in freedom, egalitarianism, autonomy, and the ideal of individual ownership of land. After two centuries, these rights and privileges have not been fully extended to Americans from all cultural, social, and economic backgrounds, however.

BACKGROUND AND THESIS

Thomas Jefferson and his political allies idealized the yeoman farmer as a republican citizen and a stalwart defender of liberty. While Jefferson undoubtedly overstated the moral virtues of the average Virginia freeholder, he did not exaggerate the importance of land ownership to most freeborn Virginia men and their families. The story of "Taking Possession" tells how three interrelated forces—the attraction of private ownership of land for Virginians, Native Americans' desire to retain control of their ancestral homes, and developing imperial policies— played out during the seventeenth and eighteenth centuries. Competition for the possession of land and resources changed both Europeans and Indians and led to the formation of a number of fundamental American values.

From the earliest years of English settlement, the promise of land ownership lured a steady stream of European immigrants to Virginia. That inducement increased in the opening years of the eighteenth century. The quest for new land to cultivate fueled the spread of colonial settlement from the Tidewater, first to the Piedmont and then into the Southside. Settlers from Pennsylvania moved into the Shenandoah Valley. Finally, Virginians pushed into the Ohio River Valley and Kentucky. During the seventeenth century, Virginians developed a means to acquire land that they repeated again and again as they settled farther westward. It began with the development of a foothold, a fort or trading post, from which to begin the exploration and mapping of the new land and its resources. As a first step in taking possession, settlers often abandoned Indian names in favor of familiar English ones. Next, a system of acquisition developed that legalized land ownership both for individuals planning to farm and for land companies. The land was surveyed and divided into plots. Plat maps showing boundary lines brought order to the landscape. Land thus became a commodity that could be sold to anyone who had the money to buy it. As colonists pushed westward, land in the settled areas continued to be worked for maximum profit at the expense of African labor. In the process, the environment and economy were forever altered for the economic benefit of the individual freeholders.

In their eagerness to claim the land, Virginians repeatedly came into contact, and frequently into conflict, with the native inhabitants who had an equally powerful desire to hold onto it. For the native peoples, the land and its traditional uses were at the center of their cultural identities. For colonists, land ownership was vital to their economic independence and the social advancement of their families. As settlement spread to new areas and the two groups confronted each other, their relationship usually passed through several stages. Initially, small numbers of colonists coexisted peacefully with their Indian neighbors. As exploration of the environment continued and knowledge of native groups increased, accommodations for trade evolved and

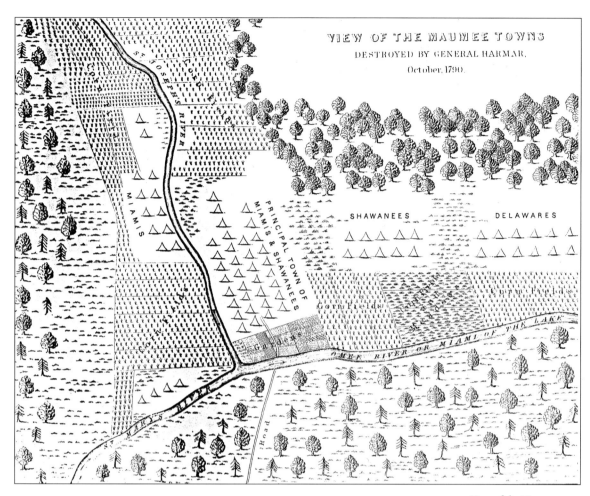

VIEW OF THE MAUMEE TOWNS
DESTROYED BY GENERAL HARMAR,
October, 1790.

View of the Maumee Towns, from *Military Journal of Major Ebenezer Denny,* 1859. Courtesy, Historical Society of Pennsylvania, Philadelphia, Pa. Major Ebenezer Denny described Miami, Shawnee, and Delaware towns on the upper Maumee River as being surrounded by "vast fields of corn in almost every direction." Like the Powhatans 170 years earlier, Ohio Country Indians were highly skilled agriculturalists.

expanded. Continuing settlement and growth of the European population required the negotiation of formalized rules of conduct and behavior to minimize conflicts. Often these efforts failed, hostilities developed, and confrontations deteriorated into armed conflict. Finally, sometimes after years of resistance, native inhabitants, such as some Tidewater Indians in the 1660s, chose to live on reservations set up for them on marginal land, or they moved farther west onto lands beyond the control of European settlers.

The developing process for land acquisitions and the evolving relationships with the native populations were shaped by unfolding policies of both imperial and colonial governments. Beginning in the fifteenth and sixteenth centuries, European empires expressed their rationales for colonization of the New World, legitimized their land claims based on exploration, the church, and conquest, and set goals for settling their new lands. Each European power (Spain, France, Netherlands, England) provided varying degrees of support for these efforts and established its own system of administrative control. As the commercial and strategic value of their colonies grew, Europeans perceived a greater need to protect their interests, so changes occurred in the areas of law and bureaucracy. Imperial governments also had to cope with a number of conflicting interests—those of the mother country, the colonists, and the Indians. Boundary disputes between colonies and the conflicting land claims that resulted had to be resolved. Finally, the rivalry between imperial powers over claims in the New World had to be settled. This usually necessitated the use of military force. After the British acquired French territory by conquest in 1763, the trans-Appalachian area was opened up to colonial settlement.

Virginia's colonial government based in Williamsburg acted to support the interests of both the mother country and the colony in land acquisition and in relationships with Indians. Although the governor was the Crown's representative, he was also the advocate for the colony. He had to mediate among the various local interest groups as well as push his own agenda. Assisting in these multiple roles was the Council. The House of Burgesses and the courts legalized the system to protect public and private property, provided a way to work out differences, and oversaw public investment in economic development.

CROSS-CULTURAL INTERACTION

When the first Englishmen stepped ashore in Virginia, they entered an intentionally managed landscape but, because it bore little resemblance to what they had left behind, they failed to recognize it. As farmers, Indians throughout Virginia centered life, in part, around their cleared fields; as hunters, they also ranged widely across their land in search of game. Indians jealously guarded the land they considered theirs, yet no one owned it. The land was thought to be alive spiritually. It could be used, but not possessed, by humans. The English settlers of Virginia were also an agrarian people for whom the land was just as important. Through husbandry, the land would yield its fruits. Yet for the English, the land had an intrinsic value beyond what it produced. It was a commodity to be owned and exploited, and its accumulation conveyed wealth and status on its owner. Although most Africans who came to Virginia could not own land legally, like the Indians, they found English concepts of land ownership unfamiliar; they were accustomed to a different legal system and held land communally. Nevertheless, Africans did take possession of the land in a very real sense. With the labor they invested by working it and by creating meaningful landmarks, Africans reassembled a recognizable landscape as a stabilizing constant in their lives.

Much of the tension inherent in the relationship between the Indians and the English stemmed from their different concepts of land ownership. Indians never internalized the European concept, and, where they were nu-

The Town of Secota, by Theodore de Bry, engraving, 1590. Europeans did not always agree that the Indians' managed landscape was the proper way to use the environment.

Delaware and Mohican Indians Baptized. Courtesy, Rare Book Division, New York Public Library, New York, N. Y., Astor, Lenox, and Tilden Foundations. Moravian missionaries baptized Delaware and Mohican Indians in Bethlehem, Pa., early in the eighteenth century.

merous enough to enforce the rules of their own culture, they simply refused to acknowledge it. At first, the English colonists equated Indians and their nonproprietary views with squatters who occupied the land but had no real claim to it. Because the Indians did not farm as they did, the English saw mostly an empty land fairly begging to be "properly" cultivated. In time, Virginians and British officials came to recognize Indians' claims to the land and sought formal land cessions from them, yet Virginians never abandoned their view that Indians occupied territory properly intended for English settlement.

The Powhatan Indians warily tolerated the presence of the first English who arrived in Virginia. Perhaps the Powhatans hoped to gain an advantage over their Indian neighbors through trade or military alliance with the European intruders. However, their unease grew as increasing numbers of colonists began to settle permanently in Virginia. Apprehension quickly turned to alarm when the English appropriated the cleared fields upon which the Indians' agriculture depended. Sporadic violence gave way to open warfare in the early 1620s as the Powhatans attempted to repel the invaders who threatened their way of life. Although the Powhatans inflicted heavy casualties on the settlers, the Native Americans were unable to drive them away. The Indians lost, but they were a resilient people who adjusted to the expansion of settlement by withdrawing to areas still free of colonists. There, with a bitter knowledge of English intentions, they reestablished their traditional way of life. This pattern—the expansion of colonists into Indian territory, followed by violent confrontation and the withdrawal of the Indians—was repeated several times during Virginia's colonial history.

Many intercultural encounters were peaceful initially. Trade was the central element of their often mutually beneficial relationships. Through their encounters, Indians and colonists constructed a "middle ground" of shared cultural meanings where they could communicate and work together, at least for a time. Many Indians and Europeans circulated in this middle ground, acting as mediators and go-betweens. They included the métis who became an interpreter, the Indian convert leading a prayer service, the European trader intent upon making a profit, the white captive adoptee who preferred Indian society to his own, and the black seeking a degree of freedom outside the effective reach of colonial authority. Even on this common ground few, if any, achieved complete understanding of the other's culture. Indians and colonists continued to view each other warily, and conflict frequently lurked just beneath the surface of apparent harmony. Conflicting claims to the land often brought latent hostilities into the open. Unfortunately, violence frequently resulted. Leaders on both sides tried to diffuse and limit disturbances through formal treaties, but neither Englishmen nor Indians had much success in binding their people to such agreements for long. The extreme xenophobia each group felt toward the other, and especially the enmity frontier colonists displayed toward Indians, doomed most treaties to failure. In the end, Europeans turned to the provincial and British military to regulate colonial settlement and then to suppress Indian resistance.

LAND ACQUISITION

As Indians slowly withdrew from the Tidewater or retreated onto the few reservations allotted them, the colonists gained possession of a vast territory east of the Blue Ridge free of native opposition. The richness and abundance of this land attracted the attention of acquisitive settlers, and the system of individual land acquisition established by colonial officials was well suited to fulfill the desires of the most aggressive land seeker. The Virginia land patent system in the seventeenth century was based on the headright, which rewarded those who imported labor to work the tobacco fields with grants of

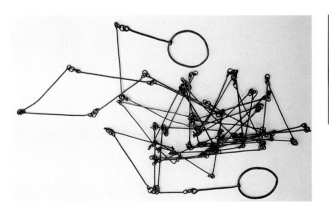

Survey chain.

Survey compass.

land. The use of treasury rights to claim land in the eighteenth century was even better suited for expansive land acquisition.

The method by which Virginia colonists took possession of the land once the Indians were forced to relinquish their claims to it was institutionalized in the "Charters, Laws and Custom of Virginia." The land grant process with its surveys, plats, and patents imposed a semblance of order on the scramble to find new, fresh land to cultivate. Once a title was conveyed, marked trees set forth the metes and bounds of the property for other colonists to respect. The regular processioning sponsored by Anglican parishes renewed the boundary marks and reconfirmed their location in the memory of the neighborhood. Boundary disputes were to be resolved first by an appeal to neighbors. If that failed, the parties could argue their case before the county court. The application of English common law, combined with circumstances

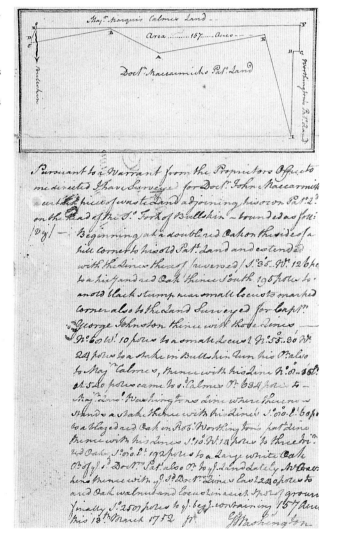

A Survey for 157 Acres. George Washington drew this plat for Dr. John MacCormick on March 13, 1752. Plats that set forth the metes and bounds of a tract of land were required before a patent could be issued.

peculiar to Virginia like the more equitable distribution of land among heirs, highlighted the central importance of land and created formidable protections for the claims of Virginia landowners.

The resale of patented tracts made for an active land market throughout the colonial period. Even in the mid-eighteenth century, land trading never completely stopped in the long-settled Tidewater. However, since planters could not continue to subdivide their land into ever smaller plots and still maintain a viable, profitable plantation, the availability of cheap land diminished over time. Consequently, land seekers turned their attention to west and southwest Virginia where speculators with vast tracts of land often clashed with land-hungry frontier settlers. These confrontations failed to slow colonial expansion, and by the 1750s, Virginians were again encountering powerful native groups who contested colonists' claims to the land. The seeming freedom with which land could be acquired created the expectation that most freeborn Virginians could own it. In fact, after a century and a half of experience, they had come to believe that land ownership was a right that could not be abridged.

As white Virginians moved westward, they took their slaves with them. Africans who could not participate in the promise of land ownership did make the land their own. Beneath the ordered landscape that freeholding Virginians created, African-Virginians imposed a far different structure on the land. Paths through the woods and fields hidden from view, rather than roads to church and court, linked slave quarters and helped maintain economic and familial slave networks. Slaves saw deep ravines and inaccessible swamps—useless to white planters—as welcome refuges for those seeking escape. Woods preserved by free planters for fuel and timber became, at night, the source of game that supplemented meager slave rations. Quiet glades and glens became social gathering spots. African-Virginians invested the physical world with rich, often deeply spiritual, meanings.

By the end of the seventeenth century, English officials had grown alarmed at the rampant corruption in Virginia's land grant system and instituted reforms to correct the worst of the abuses that had so benefited the colony's largest planters. Yet imperial neglect and the intransigence of Virginia's elite rendered reforms ineffectual. Except for occasional complaints about shortfalls in royal revenues, imperial administrators did not seriously reexamine Virginia's land policies until the mid-eighteenth century, and until the 1760s, the system for acquiring land in the colony clearly favored those Virginians whose great wealth enabled them to claim thousands of acres at a time. Since the gentry also monopolized Virginia's high political offices, they were often in the best position to claim the choicest land.

In an effort to profit from their investments, speculators divided their holdings into smaller tracts that they willingly offered for sale to new arrivals.

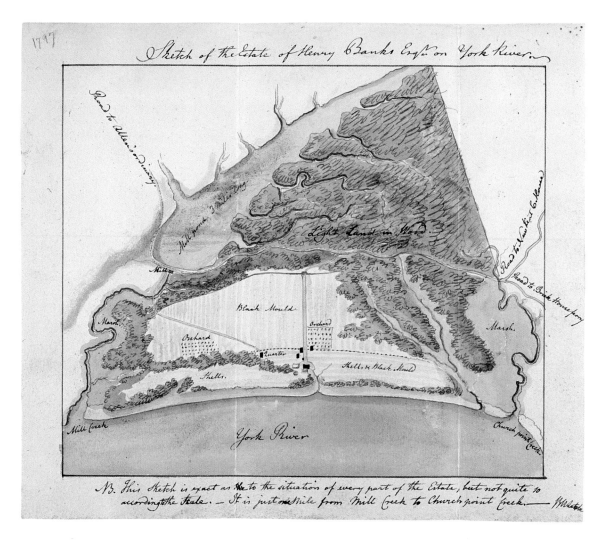

Sketch of the Estate of Henry Banks Esqr. on York River, by Benjamin Latrobe, pen and ink and watercolor, Virginia [1797]. Courtesy, Historical Society of Pennsylvania, Philadelphia, Pa. The road to New Kent courthouse linked the whites on the plantation to a wider world, while the plantation's black residents knew the surrounding creeks, swamps, and woods intimately.

Although the numbers of large-scale speculators increased during the eighteenth century, many colonists of more modest means continued to claim smaller grants for western land. Landless tenants became a permanent feature of the social landscape in the older, longer-settled region of the colony, however. Most poor whites and free blacks could not afford to move to where land was still relatively cheap.

During much of the seventeenth century, England and France paid scant attention to the territorial aspirations of their migrating nationals. Each nation maintained its sovereign claims to the New World, but focused its imperial concerns on colonial trade. As the colonies grew and expanded, the issue of imperial sovereignty over the New World, especially the trans-Appalachian West, came to the fore. When victory in the Seven Years' War resolved the issue in Great Britain's favor, the mother country had to balance Indian interests, the desires of provincial expansionists, and its own imperial goals as never before. British authorities now faced aggressive land companies poised to exploit millions of acres west of the Appalachians, defiant Indians opposed to their intrusion, and the high cost of maintaining peace on the frontier. In 1763, they banned settlement west of the Appalachians until formal boundaries between the Indians and the colonies could be negotiated. Even after a boundary line was drawn, Virginians still were prohibited from taking up land in the ceded territory. Finally, in 1774, Great Britain ordered the implementation of a radical new land grant system to replace the one Virginia had employed since the early seventeenth century. These actions added to the large-scale speculators' grievances against the British ministry but did little to hold back the flood of small farmers lured west by the promise of "open" land.

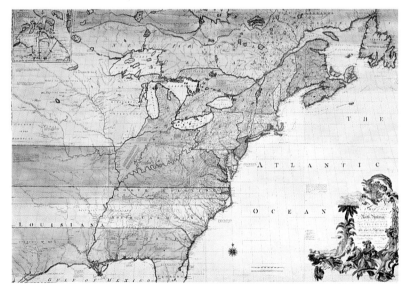

This 1755 map by John Mitchell shows the vast new territory Great Britain obtained from France as a result of victory in the French and Indian War. The availability of new land beyond the Appalachian Mountains increased tensions among the colonists, the mother country, and the Native Americans.

*Thomas Walker (1715–
1794) of Albemarle
County, Virginia,*
silhouette. Courtesy,
Manuscripts Depart-
ment, University of
Virginia Library,
Charlottesville, Va.

WILLIAMSBURG'S CENTRAL ROLE

Beginning with Jamestown, the capital of Virginia played a key role in
the acquisition of land and in the relationships between Virginians and Native Americans. Laws dealing with land acquisition, Indian trade, and internal defense were debated and passed in the House of Burgesses and the Council.
When the colony's capital was moved to Williamsburg, the newly created
capital, in 1699, English settlement had yet to penetrate into the Piedmont.
The hundreds of Indians still living in the Tidewater region no longer troubled
the Virginia colonists.

Although Virginians had barely begun to claim their portion of the
New World by 1700, the colony's ancient charter did encompass a vast territory extending to the Ohio River Valley and beyond. Within its far-flung
borders awaited large and powerful native groups undergoing stressful reor-
ganization. In addition, the French in Canada acted to increase their influence south into the Ohio Country. Western Virginia was to become a contested
area. As Virginians pushed into it, Williamsburg, the colonial capital, became the nerve center in which policies were developed and implemented to
ensure orderly expansion. Government officials in Williamsburg directed diplomatic initiatives toward the Saponis and Nottoways in the 1710s and 1720s,
the Catawbas and Cherokees in the 1750s and 1760s, the Delawares and
Shawnees in the 1760s and 1770s, and, throughout the period, the Iroquois.
In Williamsburg, the governor—as the Crown's representative—attempted
to balance his own and imperial goals toward western lands against the special provincial interests of the colony's powerful elite and yeomanry. Gover-
nors Spotswood, Dinwiddie, Fauquier, Botetourt, and Dunmore all took active
roles in westward expansion and treated with numerous Indian diplomatic
missions to Williamsburg.

Traces of the old palisade that passed through Williamsburg could still
be seen in the eighteenth century, reminding those who reflected on it that
Indians and Englishmen had very different understandings of what it meant
to "own" land. The palisade had been built early in the seventeenth century to
bar Indians from the area of English settlement because the Indians refused
to acknowledge they were trespassing when they hunted on land "owned" by
the English. The remnant of the palisade trench confirmed that, for colonists, land was meant to be confined within boundaries and fences. The Cherokee delegation that crossed the old palisade line on their way to meet with
Lord Botetourt in August 1770 had thoroughly learned the language of European property ownership. As they negotiated the location of a fixed boundary between Cherokee and English settlement, they assumed that any English
found beyond the line would be "trespassing" on Indian land and could be
forced to leave.

News of the frontier arrived often in the capital. Traders, interpreters,

Alexander Spotswood, by Charles Bridges, oil on canvas, America, 1736-1750.

land speculators, and surveyors met in Williamsburg and discussed various issues of importance to Virginia's expansionism. Christopher Gist, commissioned by Governor Dinwiddie to act as an agent for the Ohio Company to the Indian Treaty held at Logstown in 1752, explored much of the Ohio Country and visited Williamsburg to report on his travels. Burgesses for the western counties debated issues of expansionism with the more conservative members from the Tidewater counties. One such burgess, Thomas Walker from Albemarle County, was an explorer, a member of the Loyal Land Company, and a colonial agent who had numerous dealings with the Indians. County surveyors were licensed at the College of William and Mary. Many colonists claiming unpatented land had to go to the land office in Williamsburg to have their claim officially recorded. William Parks printed the Treaty of Lancaster in 1744; twelve years later, William Hunter published the treaty between a Virginia delegation commissioned by Governor Dinwiddie and the Catawbas and Cherokees.

Numerous Indians visited or even lived for awhile in Williamsburg during the eighteenth century. Indian delegations met with the governor, councillors, and other leading citizens at the Palace and Capitol. They held ceremonies on Market Square where individual Mattaponis and Pamunkeys sold wild fowl and pottery on market days. Beginning in the early eighteenth century, a steady number of Indian youngsters enrolled in the the Brafferton School at the College of William and Mary. Their teachers hoped to "enlighten" them about English ways so that they could return to their homes and help "civilize" their people. Few fulfilled the faculty's expectations, and many returned to their traditional ways once they went home. Some, like Catawba John Nettles, put their English schooling to good use and became successful interpreters and mediators between the Indians and the colonists. Nettles's William and Mary education helped the Catawbas maintain their cultural autonomy in what for them was a hostile world. Similarly, John Montour, the son of métis interpreter Andrew Montour, followed in his father's footsteps after his years at the college.

When Lord Dunmore arrived in Virginia, he quickly allied himself with the colony's expansion-minded elite. Acting with the advice of his Council, he sparred with Pennsylvania over control of the Monongahela River Valley. However, his great ambition was to force a cession of the Kentucky territory from the Shawnees and other Ohio Country Indians. Through the spring and early summer of 1774, Dunmore eagerly awaited news from the frontier. A reported raid by Logan, an Ohio Iroquois, to revenge his family's murder was just the pretense Dunmore needed to mount a massive invasion of the Ohio Country. Plans for the operation, which he personally led, so preoccupied his thoughts that he paid little attention to the pending First Virginia Convention. He had left town when it met in Williamsburg in August.

Dunmore was not so distracted that he failed to attend the Council's June meetings at which caveats received in the past year were reviewed. Caveats put a stop to the granting of a land patent until rival claims to the same tract could be heard. The caveat court held in Williamsburg was just a part of the elaborate land system that had developed by the 1770s to regulate and protect the rights of landowners.

Dunmore's war ended in victory. During the resulting treaty negotiations, Logan's address to Dunmore signaled his reluctant acceptance of defeat. When the governor and four young Shawnee hostages returned to Williamsburg in December, they were greeted with loud public acclaim. The hostages returned to the Ohio Country in June 1775, carrying with them news of the political disarray among the Virginians.

By the time Logan's speech was published in the *Virginia Gazette* in early 1775, it had already been circulating in Williamsburg for several weeks. The speech was a topic of conversation among gentlemen gathered at the city's taverns, and students were instructed to copy it as an exercise. Jefferson and many others who read the speech in Williamsburg admired its eloquence. Like Jefferson, some saw it as evidence of the Indians' nobility. But other voices were also heard. Graphic and sensational stories of Indian atrocities against western settlers circulated among city residents whenever frontier news reached the governor or was published in the newspapers. Nevertheless, Logan's speech touched a nerve. His tale of one Indian's efforts at accommodation, his angry reaction to betrayal by whites, and his ultimate loss of family, land, and spirit captured the essence of the encounter of Indians and colonists. The continuing nineteenth-century popularity of Logan's speech may have come from its appeal to those uneasy with the human cost of America's unceasing march westward.

Kanagagota (Standing Turkey)—"Old Hopp of Chote," by Francis Parsons, oil on canvas, London, 1762. Courtesy, Gilcrease Museum, Tulsa, Okla.

Slave trader, Sold to Tennessee, by Lewis Miller, watercolor and ink on paper, Virginia, 1853–1867. The constant movement westward had its price—the loss of Indian autonomy and lands and the expansion of slavery. These slaves were being moved from Stanton, Va., to Tennessee.

LEGACY

Although most colonial Virginians who owned land acquired it in routine ways—by patent, purchase, or inheritance—the memory of violent struggles to wrest control of the land from the Indians, coupled with reports of the bloody contest in the West in the 1760s and 1770s, transformed the actual settlement and expansion of the colony into an epic story on the eve of the American Revolution. For many Virginians, the first colonists, and by extension current ones, attained heroic stature as they struggled against great odds to establish a society in a hostile and dangerous New World. That they succeeded in creating what many colonial Virginians described as a republic of freeholders only enhanced the significance and defining power of the story. An inevitable consequence of this interpretation was that it linked the continued success of the republican experiment to the continuing expansion of freehold settlements. While this "manifest destiny," as it developed in the nineteenth century, did celebrate democratic republicanism, it necessarily placed those already living in the West who resisted its imperative in the role of outcasts who deserved to be swept aside.

The colonists' relentless pursuit of new lands to settle obviously worked to the disadvantage of the Indians who were forced to retreat. But it would be a mistake to see the Indians as merely the broken victims of the inevitable march of history. Until the French were forced to abandon their claim to Canada and the trans-Appalachian West in 1763, Indians, most notably the Iroquois, skillfully played the imperial powers off against each other to enhance the Native Americans' importance. Others, such as the Leni-Lenapes (or Delawares) in the seventeenth century and the Cherokees in the eighteenth, masterfully exploited the rivalries between colonies to their own advantage. Even retreat was not always a prelude to a tribe's cultural collapse. The several small coastal Carolina tribes who regrouped in the Carolina uplands with the Catawbas in the early eighteenth century, the scattered Shawnees who reassembled in the Ohio Country in the 1760s, and the Delawares who relocated there from eastern Pennsylvania all experienced a cultural resurgence in their new homes that made them vigorous opponents of colonial expansion.

Indians remained powerful in the Ohio Country until after the American Revolution. With the end of the war, the United States could turn its attention to resolving lingering land disputes between Virginia and its neighbors and removing the Indians from the Ohio Territory. After the Ohio Indians were defeated at Fallen Timbers (1794), this vast land could be settled according to the provisions of the Northwest Ordinance of 1787 that established the pattern of settlement for all western lands. While the cycle of conflict, broken treaties, warfare, and eventual removal continued throughout the nineteenth century, Native Americans remained culturally resilient. One of the legacies of the broken treaties has been a number of court cases in the late twentieth century to redress these grievances. Today, Indian tribes maintain a special relationship with the federal government to the frustration of states and localities.

With the opening of the Ohio Country to American settlement, the issue of free trade down the Mississippi through New Orleans took on new importance, and relations with Spain became a significant part of the foreign policy of the United States. Jefferson's Louisiana Purchase (1803) opened vast new lands for settlement. Later in the nineteenth century, wars with Mexico and Spain added additional territory. After the settlement of the continental United States in the nineteenth century, America struggled to maintain a special interest in the Philippines, Mexico, Latin America, and the Caribbean Islands in the twentieth century. As a result of this expansionism, the Philippines became an independent nation, Alaska and Hawaii joined the United States, and the debate over the admittance of Puerto Rico as the fifty-first state continues.

The Death of General Wolfe, by Benjamin West, oil on canvas, England, 1770. Courtesy, National Gallery of Canada, Ottawa. The Indian in the foreground represents an ally of the British.

The ideal of a republic of freeholders and the conviction that it was America's "manifest destiny" to populate the entire continent fostered the belief that land and resources were unlimited. Mythic frontier values of freedom, egalitarianism, autonomy, and the ideal of individual land ownership reinforced European ideals of individualism and became part of our American heritage. The dream of owning one's home is seen today as the entitlement of all Americans, although many find it a difficult dream to realize. A final irony resulted from linking freedom to land. Some Americans equated the right to own property of all types with the right to own slaves. In fact, slavery was permitted south of the Ohio. Other Americans strongly disagreed with the concept of slavery and its continued expansion into new southwestern territories. The question would not be settled until a bloody civil war was fought during the mid-nineteenth century.

View on the Ohio River, by Benjamin Latrobe, watercolor on paper, undated [March 1815]. Courtesy, Historical Society of Pennsylvania, Philadelphia, Pa. The Ohio River became the highway by which tens of thousands of settlers flowed into Kentucky and the Northwest Territory.

"Taking Possession" and the "Becoming Americans" Theme

Diverse People

The protagonists of the "Taking Possession" story were the diverse native inhabitants of eastern North America, the several European states (principally England, France, and Spain) who asserted imperial sovereignty over the continent, and the settlers of European background and the Africans they forcibly brought to the colony who took up residence in colonial Virginia. An evolving cast of characters first featured Englishmen (and a few women), Powhatans, and Africans of West Indian backgrounds. Later, French Huguenots, Ulster Irish, Germans, Scots, and Africans joined with colonial-born Virginians, white and black, as they all encountered Iroquois, Catawbas, Delawares, Cherokees, Shawnees, and other tribes on the eve of independence.

Clashing Interests

Each group invested the land they occupied with meaning, which in turn shaped their behavior toward it. For the Indians, the land was to be used for the common good and its control guaranteed Indian cultural identity and autonomy. For the European settlers, the land was to be made productive and valuable and its ownership meant economic and social security. For African-Virginians, the land was secretly given a reassuring presence that helped them rebuild their lives. For European powers, overseas colonies enhanced national prestige and added to a country's wealth. So different in fundamental ways, these various interests coexisted uneasily. White Virginians judged the Indians' use of the land to be wasteful and unproductive. Indians condemned the whites' use of the land as selfish and destructive. African-Virginians simply ignored those boundary markers their masters imposed on the land that did not conform to their mental landscape. European nations regularly challenged each others' claims to New World territory. These tensions often gave way to violence.

Shared Values

Although the huge landholdings amassed by rich and powerful Virginians forced many poorer colonists to purchase land from speculators, to patent less desirable land, or to remain tenants, the seemingly limitless land free for the taking in the New World instilled in nearly all free Virginians, white and black, the goal of becoming freeholders. Even the majority of African-Virginians, who by necessity had to view the land only as the place where they lived and labored, understood that the land they occupied was a commodity to be bought and sold with little regard for their opinion. By the mid-eighteenth century, Indians were using the language of land ownership to defend their claims to lands beyond the edge of Virginia settlement. Yet the Indians never internalized the concept of private land ownership as had the colonial settlers of European, and, to a lesser extent African, backgrounds. Their open disdain of this ideal effectively distanced Indians from whites. Furthermore, Great Britain, where land ownership was equally a goal, failed to understand how the achievement of a freehold by a relatively large number of freemen in British terms worked to undermine colonialism.

FORMATIVE INSTITUTIONS

The friction caused by the incessant quest for land was regulated in many formal and informal arenas. A wide variety of informal contacts frequently centered around trade brought Native Americans and European and African colonists together. Although such encounters often produced misunderstandings that heightened tensions, they also created a middle ground where conversations (if not accommodations) could occur. In addition, Indian leaders and English government officials engaged in formal negotiations to resolve disputes over trade and land and to set standards for behavior. The land claims of individual Virginians were also settled through formal and informal means. Land patents were recorded in the colony's land office, courts adjudicated challenges to land titles, and neighbors walked around each other's lands to reestablished their boundaries. Although in general the haves were favored over the have-nots, Virginia's formal and informal institutions did help to guard the sanctity of private property. Even Great Britain's centuries-long and finally victorious defense of its New World claims legitimized individual British colonists' pursuit of land. Unfortunately for Great Britain, its victory also planted the seeds of Virginia's eventual independence.

PARTIAL FREEDOMS

Only hindsight allows the conquest of the Indians to seem inevitable since, at that time, the final outcome was frequently in doubt. In fact, the Indians' fierce defense of their homelands caused white Virginians to cast their struggle with the Indians in heroic terms: "Their [Virginians'] own blood was spilt in acquiring lands for their settlement . . . For themselves they fought, for themselves they conquered, and for themselves alone they have right to hold" (Thomas Jefferson). The system developed for acquiring and owning land that held sway until the 1770s clearly benefited rich colonists. Their wealth enabled them to patent thousands of the choicest acres at a time. Furthermore, the legal system protected the landowner from the land seeker. The system was hardly a closed one, however. From an Old World perspective, it was fairly open; thousands of Virginia freemen who might never have hoped to own land in England or Europe became freeholders in the colony. In the older, longer settled counties, landless tenants—mostly poor whites and free blacks—did become a common fixture. Even there, however, the promise of an eventual freehold camouflaged the dismal prospects of the landless.

REVOLUTIONARY PROMISE

The abundance of land in the heart of the new nation served as a magnet to Europe's and Asia's poor. Lured by the promise of a better life, wave after wave of immigrants from such places as Ireland, Germany, Poland, Russia, Italy, China, and Japan arrived in the United States in the nineteenth and twentieth centuries. Many died in urban tenements or work camps without realizing their dreams, but enough settled on farms or found productive work to keep the dream alive. As the tens of thousands of immigrants set about creating a new life for themselves, the reality of their accomplishments transformed the republic into a democracy. In their wake grew a hopefulness and optimism that seemed to confirm the nation's destiny as a land of freedom and opportunity, but it should not be forgotten that this belief came at a high cost. Those Americans who failed to become sturdy, independent yeomen were often wrongly stigmatized as weak and morally inferior. The Indians and the Spanish of the Southwest who rightly protested their prior claims to North America's lands were viewed with contempt by many Americans. When these "outsiders" resisted the takeover of their homes, they were frequently suppressed brutally. On balance, however, the promise of self-reliance and self-sufficiency that came along with land ownership transcended these wrongs and, over time, extended to all Americans.

CONNECTIONS TO OTHER "BECOMING AMERICANS" STORY LINES

ENSLAVING VIRGINIA

By providing a permanent labor force that could be denied the true value of their work, the system of slavery enabled many colonial Virginia slave owners to farm large tracts of land profitably. In turn, the generous land patents the Virginia grandees favored fueled westward expansion. Thus, while few blacks enjoyed the privilege of land ownership, they were inextricably tied to the quest for land well into the nineteenth century. The resulting encounters of African-Virginians and Indians produced a complex balancing act in response to whites' heavy pressure on each group to view the other with suspicion and contempt.

REDEFINING FAMILY

The general availability of land in Virginia made traditional English inheritance practices unnecessary. Oldest sons no longer stood to be principal heirs of the family land. Instead, most sons either shared in the landed inheritance or could strike out on their own with a realistic prospect of economic independence. In either case, the strength of the patriarch was weakened. Where slaves were linked to the land they worked, the relative stability of the slave community fostered the formation of families among African-Americans. Indian families were also affected. The colonists' way west was eased by the devastating effects of European diseases and by the commerce that preceded settlement. Family networks decimated by disease and the demands of trade forced many Indian societies to reassess the traditional roles of men and women and husbands and wives.

BUYING RESPECTABILITY

The Indian trade that secured for European markets such fashionable items as beaver skins for hats and deerskins for clothing inexorably linked the Indians to an emerging capitalistic market economy. The dependence of Indians on European goods that resulted enriched colonial traders and endangered traditional Indian culture. The wealth gained from trade and from other commercial ventures was often used to acquire land in large enough quantities to form the landed estates upon which the trappings of gentry gentility rested. In Virginia and the South, the labor required to make the land profitable enough to support colonists' conspicuous consumption firmly fixed slavery as an essential aspect of the economy.

CHOOSING REVOLUTION

The middling planters' relatively easy access to land linked their interests to those of the elite who dominated Virginia politics. When the gentry's powers were challenged by Great Britain about 1760, they successfully convinced the yeomanry that their rights were challenged too. Ironically, the revolutionaries' rhetoric about freedom and the sanctity of property engendered in some slaves (that special "species of property") an equally strong desire for freedom. That desire moved many African-Virginians to take up arms against their former masters. The American Revolution forced all Indian groups in close contact with the colonists to choose which side they would support; neutrality was not an option. A few, like the Catawbas, sided with the colonists but gained little credit for their decision. Others, such as the Iroquois, found themselves irrevocably split: most of the Oneidas sided with the Americans while the majority of the remaining Iroquois supported the British. The controversy ultimately destroyed all that they had worked to preserve since the early 1700s. By 1800, the few Indians who remained in New York were confined to a handful of small reservations. The League has remained divided between Canada and New York ever since.

FREEING RELIGION

Virginia's westward expansion depended, in part, on the colony's ability to attract large numbers of new settlers. The settlers who flocked to the Virginia backcountry were an ethnically diverse group with religious beliefs at variance with the colony's Anglican establishment. These newcomers demanded respect for their beliefs. Their quest eventually moved beyond toleration to insistence on complete religious freedom. The greater emotional and spiritual stance of these dissenting religions found a receptive audience among a great many African-Virginians. As converts, they created a Christian faith that minimized earthly tribulations in favor of heavenly rewards. The Indians of the eighteenth century were also a religiously diverse people. Some, such as the Ottawas or the Caughnawaga Iroquois, were baptized by Jesuits and professed Catholic beliefs. Others, such as some Delawares, were newly converted by Moravian missionaries in the 1750s and 1760s. Most continued to practice their own religious traditions, however. Their beliefs, which incorporated a few elements learned from their European Christian neighbors, continued to provide Indians with spiritual strength and direction.

Story Line Team: John Caramia, Gary Brumfield, Richard Frazier, Jay Gaynor, Nancy Hagedorn, Kevin Kelly, Barbara McGowan, Robin Scouse, Tom Spear, and Robert C. Watson.

FURTHER READING

Egnal, Marc. "The Origins of the Revolution in Virginia: A Reinterpretation." *William and Mary Quarterly,* 3rd Ser., XXXVII (1980), pp. 401–428.

Hatley, Tom. *The Dividing Paths: Cherokees and South Carolinians Through the Era of Revolution.* New York: Oxford University Press, 1993.

Hinderaker, Eric. *Elusive Empires: Constructing Colonialism in the Ohio Valley, 1673–1800.* Cambridge: Cambridge University Press, 1997.

Hughes, Sarah S. *Surveyors and Statesmen: Land Measuring in Colonial Virginia.* Richmond, Va.: Virginia Association of Surveyors, 1979.

Kulikoff, Allan. *Tobacco and Slaves: The Development of Southern Cultures in the Chesapeake, 1680–1800.* Chapel Hill, N. C.: University of North Carolina Press, 1986.

McConnell, Michael N. *A Country Between: The Upper Ohio Valley and Its Peoples, 1724–1774.* Lincoln, Nebr.: University of Nebraska Press, 1992.

Merrell, James H. *The Indians' New World: Catawbas and Their Neighbors from European Contact through the Era of Removal.* Chapel Hill, N. C.: University of North Carolina Press, 1989.

Morton, Richard L. *Colonial Virginia.* Vol. II: *Westward Expansion and Prelude to Revolution, 1710–1763.* Chapel Hill, N. C.: University of North Carolina Press, 1960.

Nobles, Gregory H. "Breaking into the Backcountry: New Approaches to the Early American Frontier, 1750–1800. *"William and Mary Quarterly,* 3rd Ser., XLVI (1989), pp. 641–670.

Onuf, Peter S. *Jefferson's Empire: The Language of American Neighborhood.* Charlottesville, Va.: University Press of Virginia, 2000.

Robinson, W. Stitt. *The Southern Colonial Frontier, 1607–1763.* Albuquerque. N. Mex.: University of New Mexico Press, 1979.

Rountree, Helen C. *Pocahontas' People: The Powhatan Indians of Virginia Through Four Centuries.* Norman, Okla.: University of Oklahoma Press, 1990.

Silver, Timothy. *A New Face on the Countryside: Indians, Colonists, and Slaves in South Atlantic Forests, 1500–1800.* Cambridge: Cambridge University Press, 1990.

White, Richard. *The Middle Ground: Indians, Empires, and Republics in the Great Lakes Region, 1650–1815.* Cambridge: Cambridge University Press, 1991.

Detail from *The Death of General Wolfe,* by Benjamin West, oil on canvas, England, 1770, courtesy, National Gallery of Canada, Ottawa.

Virginia slaves worked in the tobacco fields from dawn to dusk.

ENSLAVING VIRGINIA

Medallion, by Josiah Wedgwood, unglazed stoneware, Staffordshire, England, ca. 1787.
Josiah Wedgwood, one of the founders of the Society for the Suppression of the Slave
Trade, made this medallion that features a chained, kneeling slave. It became the
emblem of the English and American abolitionist movements.

ENSLAVING VIRGINIA

The "Enslaving Virginia" story line addresses the development and growth of a racially based slave system that profoundly affected the lives, fortunes, and values of blacks and whites.

KEY POINTS

- BACKGROUND. The institution of slavery marked both black and white society in eighteenth-century Virginia. Along with the racial attitudes and class structure that developed alongside it and served to legitimate a slave system based on skin color, slavery permeated all aspects of life in the colony.

- SLAVERY TAKES ROOT AND GROWS. The demand for labor in Europe's New World possessions led to the forced migration of at least 11.5 million Africans from the sixteenth to the nineteenth centuries. Approximately 600,000 were brought into British North America. Although slave laws were enacted piecemeal in seventeenth-century Virginia, they added up to an effective system of discrimination and exploitation.

- A RACIALLY FRACTURED SOCIETY EMERGES. As the numbers of Africans in Virginia increased, the cultural differences that set them apart from Europeans and their unequal status and treatment created great divisions in Chesapeake society.

- RACIAL SLAVERY CODIFIED. Laws passed in the 1660s defined who was and was not to be enslaved, a designation that increasingly came to be attached exclusively to Africans. Over the next fifty years, still more laws restricted the movement of slaves, set harsh punishments for infractions against the system, and strengthened slaveholders' rights to their human property.

- CRACKS IN THE SYSTEM. Africans had little impact on altering formal institutions. Sometimes they could influence personal relationships with individual whites. Plantation slaves also had leeway to make choices in work groups and in local exchange networks.

- THE STRAINED WORLD BLACKS AND WHITES MADE TOGETHER. Blacks and whites had a profound effect on one another's lives and culture, however inadvertently. Their interaction colored everything from attitudes to ancestors.

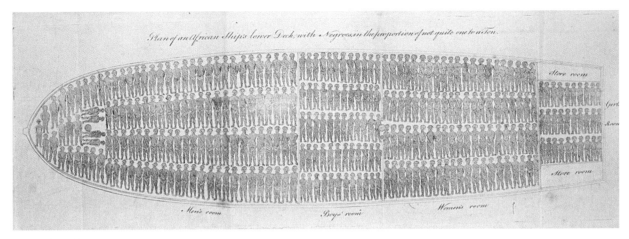

"Plan of an African Ship's lower Deck, with Negroes," engraving, Philadelphia, 1797. An American rendition of the original chart of slaves' shipboard quarters was used in the American antislavery movement.

BACKGROUND AND THESIS

A system of hereditary bondage for blacks developed gradually in the decades following the arrival of the first Africans at Jamestown by 1619. Slavery became entrenched in Virginia over the next 150 years. A series of restrictive laws reinforced by community and family mores legitimized its hold on blacks and whites alike.

Slavery—defined as the ownership and forced exploitation of one person by another—was the foundation of the agricultural system in Virginia and the cornerstone of the colony's economy. At first, planters bought slaves primarily to raise tobacco for export. By the last quarter of the eighteenth century, slave-owning farmers were using bound labor throughout the diversified agricultural economy of the region. Enslaved African-Americans also worked as skilled tradesmen in the countryside as well as in the capital city of Williamsburg. Some served as domestics in the households of wealthy white Virginians.

The frequent interaction between black slaves and white masters, and, for that matter, between blacks and whites in general, created a complex interdependence that eventually produced a distinctive hybrid culture. Relations between the races were as destructive as they were unequal. The horrors of slavery, both physical and psychological, were numerous. The system conferred a presumption of superiority on whites whether or not they were slaveholders. Economic reliance on slave labor, fears about the consequences of emancipation, and unyielding racial prejudice and cultural bias all contributed to the maintenance of slavery at the same time that whites severed the colony's bonds to Great Britain. The "Enslaving Virginia" story explains the effects of slavery and the influence of Africans on every aspect of Virginia society.

The term *African-Virginian* is used to reflect more accurately the distinct differences between the slave experience in Virginia and, to a larger extent, in the Chesapeake from that in the Carolinas or the northern colonies.

SLAVERY TAKES ROOT AND GROWS

The notion that slavery was inconsistent with the Englishman's love of liberty has long been an argument advanced by die-hard apologists. It is untenable. English settlers seldom doubted the superiority of their own customs and culture. They were quick to adopt the same exploitative policies used effectively by other European colonizers in dealing with the peoples they encountered and conquered in the New World. Their contemporaneous experience subduing the native peoples of Ireland gave them practice and precedent for the conquest of Virginia. Few Englishmen in the seventeenth century doubted that they were God's chosen instruments to bring the blessings of civilization and true religion to alien peoples who lacked both.

From the beginning, English settlers in Virginia pursued two goals primarily: to make the colony a financial success and to convert Indians to Christianity. The English regarded their possession of North America to be justified and righteous, however much it appears arrogant and immoral today. They believed they could make better use of the land and its resources than did the Indians they dispossessed. They saw it as their duty as Christians to spread the gospel "throughout the world." They were prepared to employ if possible, and to subdue if necessary, any peoples living within reach of their New World trading empire.

Cartouche from *AFRICA, According to Mr. D'Anville . . .* , by Robert Sayer, line engraving on paper with hand-colored outline, London, 1772. Despite extensive text elsewhere on the map that describes in detail the peoples, customs, trade, and natural resources of Africa, this cartouche, which portrays cannibalism, depicts how Europeans saw African culture.

Other Europeans besides the English had similar economic ambitions and held similar convictions about their own cultural and religious superiority. The Portuguese and Spanish had already colonized parts of Central and South America a century before the English gained a toehold in Virginia. Expeditions from Holland and France planted colonies in North, Central, and South America about the same time the English staked out Virginia. Seeking easy profits, Europeans grew semitropical crops—especially sugar and tobacco—for the international market. Such crops lent themselves to plantation production and the forced labor of Native American and, increasingly, African slaves. Between 1450 and 1600, European merchants and colonizers collaborated with certain rulers and merchants in West Africa to establish a regular trade in slaves. European products and New World staples changed hands for African gold, ivory, and human captives. Whereas laws in northern Europe made no provision for slavery, Spanish and Portuguese practice in the New World provided a ready model that later-arriving Dutch, French, and English colonists quickly adopted.

Shortly after the establishment of Jamestown, the Virginia Company revoked its earlier policy and advised the settlers to shun their Indian neighbors. At first, settlers had formed a mutually beneficial alliance with the Algonquin peoples of Tidewater Virginia. The Algonquins had provided the settlers food, land, and protection from more hostile Native American groups. For their part, the English became valuable trading partners to the Algonquins. Their reciprocal alliance began to crumble by the 1620s. The English settlers' insatiable desire for lands that natives were unwilling to cede often led to bloodshed. Conflicts also arose over English attempts to convert Native Americans to Christianity and efforts to enslave the Algonquins. The Virginia government banished Native Americans from white settlements after 1622 and sometimes even tried to exterminate them altogether. Never-ending guerrilla warfare between Indians and settlers, when coupled with the Virginians' practice of occasionally enslaving native captives taken in war, encouraged racial hatred. The enslavement of Africans in the following decades forced Native American groups to choose between aiding the English by helping to enforce slave laws or assisting blacks by harboring runaways.

Slavery was not unfamiliar to most Africans. Ancient African civilizations relied heavily on slave labor to perform a variety of tasks, as did many other societies throughout the course of history. The Islamic world sanctioned slavery as a legitimate strategy to convert "pagans" to the true religion. From the seventeenth century on, Arab and Muslim societies traded for slaves in northern and sub-Saharan Africa. Those from sub-Saharan Africa were used as domestic servants or as farm hands; those from North Africa as soldiers, administrators, and house slaves.

Slavery was also a fairly common practice in the kinship-based societies of West and Central Africa. Owning people was a source and a symbol of

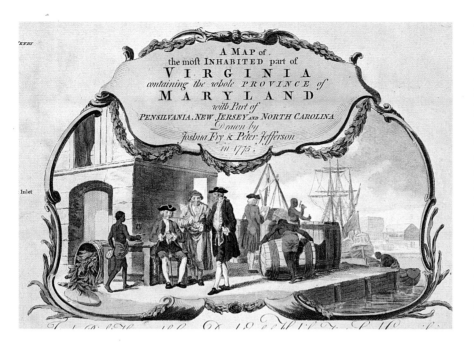

Cartouche from *A Map of the most Inhabited part of Virginia . . . ,* by Joshua Fry and Peter Jefferson, hand-colored line engraving, England, 1751. Courtesy, Swem Library, College of William and Mary, Williamsburg, Va. Free and enslaved men inspect and pack tobacco bound for a British port. Virginia's economy was based on a slave society that produced tobacco for export to foreign markets.

wealth in societies where the community, rather than individuals, held all rights to land. There, slaves were usually war captives, criminals, debtors (or their designates), and sometimes foreigners. Some were purchased for life-long servitude, while others could eventually earn their freedom. Depending on the nature of local resources, economic systems, and social and legal structures, slaves in different parts of West and Central Africa were used as agricultural laborers, miners, or porters. Others served as soldiers, clerks, concubines, or religious sacrifices. Like members of the European gentry, privileged Africans gained power, wealth, and status by controlling dependent persons— wives, children, kin, clients, subjects, and servants and slaves. African slavery was thus a part of a continuum of social relationships. Since slavery was already a way of life in several African societies, Europeans at first simply had to establish trading partnerships and alliances (by force if necessary) to tap into existing supplies of enslaved men and women. But soon entrepreneurs organized raiding parties to kidnap captives to meet the growing demand. The New World market gradually transformed traditional forms of African slavery into a capitalist enterprise.

The demand for ever-larger numbers of slaves to work New World staple crop plantations and mines led to the forced transatlantic migration of roughly 11.5 million Africans in the three centuries from 1500 to 1800. (Some estimates place the number as high as 40,000,000 to 100,000,000 to account for smuggling, poor record keeping, and higher mortality rates en route to the New World than conventional estimates project.) Almost 75 percent of enslaved Africans, the largest proportion, were taken to Central and South

America by the Portuguese and Spanish. Approximately 600,000 Africans were brought into British North America between 1619 and 1775.

Most English slave owners were interested in Africans with skills that matched their needs. They sought out farming peoples and those with metal- and woodworking skills. Despite the horrors of transportation and the burden of work they were expected to perform, Africans brought to mainland North America managed to survive far better than those who ended up in other parts of the Americas. The high rate of survival can be attributed to the more favorable epidemiological environment in British North America as contrasted with that of the Caribbean and Central and South America. It was also owing to their adaptability and resistance and to tobacco cultivation, which was less labor-intensive than sugar production. These factors also resulted in unusually high rates of natural increase, especially among creole slaves. By 1770, Africans and their American-born descendants made up 40 percent of Virginia's population. Many counties had substantial black majorities.

Most bound workers in Virginia were white indentured servants, not African slaves, until the 1680s. Thereafter, Virginia planters began purchasing significantly larger numbers of Africans to supplement and eventually to replace dwindling supplies of English and Irish servants willing to work in the tobacco fields. So long as blacks were a small minority of the Chesapeake population (before 1690, Africans and their descendants made up no more than 7 percent of the population in Virginia and Maryland), black and white laborers usually worked side by side in the fields, ate and socialized together, shared living quarters, and, in some cases, formed mixed race families.

Most blacks, but not all, were bought and sold as chattel slaves. Early on, the circumstances in which transported Africans arrived in the Chesapeake colonies often determined their subsequent status as bondsmen for life or occasionally as free blacks. Between the mid-1660s and the early eighteenth century, the Virginia legislature strengthened the laws that gave planters the right to hold Africans and their descendants as lifelong slaves. These laws reinforced the equation between slaves' bondage and their African ancestry. The legal status of a person of mixed race was determined by his or her mother's race and status. These legal changes made slaves a more attractive investment despite their higher initial sale price.

Until the last quarter of the seventeenth century, many men and women from West Africa were transported to the Chesapeake by way of the West Indies rather than directly from Africa. For some, the islands were a brief stopping place on the forced journey from Africa. Others had labored on Caribbean plantations before they were resold to masters on the mainland. Others were island born. These earliest Africans and their West Indies-born children, especially those from societies long involved in the transatlantic slave trade, were familiar with Europeans. They knew their languages, customs, and religions. Some of them, former middlemen, were personally acquainted with the European slave trade. They drew on this knowledge and on their skills at intercultural negotiation to blunt slaves' abuse and debasement by their New World masters. They knowingly cultivated patrons and embraced mediating institutions such as churches to improve their chances and to establish a place for themselves in a still ill-defined social order. Attempts to tame their oppressors' political and economic institutions proved difficult at best and mostly ineffectual. Surer successes were those that individual slaves negotiated directly with their owners.

A slave is being offered to the highest bidder at a modern-day re-creation of a public sale.

Adult slaves passed occupational skills and important cultural knowledge on to the next generation.

A RACIALLY FRACTURED SOCIETY EMERGES

Slave traders brought approximately 54,000 blacks to Virginia and Maryland from 1700 to 1740. The majority were sold to planters in a few lower Tidewater counties, including York and James City, adjacent to Williamsburg. Many forced migrants came from the inland areas of Ibo-speaking West Africa. They were mostly peoples who had had little or no contact with transatlantic trade and European cultures. Transported to the Chesapeake, they found themselves in an alien land where languages, landscape, climate, diseases, and other peoples were utterly unfamiliar. Olaudah Equiano, an African who wrote a narrative of his homeland, capture, and enslavement, described his first encounter with the European slave traders. Equiano remembered, "I was now persuaded that I had gotten into a world of bad spirits . . . . When I looked round the ship too, and saw a large furnace of copper boiling, and a multitude of black people of every description chained together, every one of their countenances expressing dejection and sorrow, I no longer doubted my fate . . . I asked them if we were not to be eaten by those white men with horrible looks, red faces, and long hair."

To white Virginians, raw Africans seemed outlandish, godforsaken, and unruly. Masters set about "taming" them by giving them new names and enforcing their use. Writing to his overseer in 1727, Robert "King" Carter gave specific instructions for renaming newly acquired slaves: Take "care that the negroes both men & women I sent . . . always go by ye names we gave them." Slaveholders also punished slaves who tried to maintain traditional African cultural customs or observed their native religious practices. Most were put to work doing repetitive and backbreaking agricultural labor. Slave drivers often used the newly arrived Africans' ignorance of English and their resistance to enslavement as excuses for imposing harsher discipline and more stringent work rules.

White servants became an increasingly distinct minority among bound laborers by the 1730s. Improving economic conditions at home stemmed the flow of bound immigrants from the British Isles. White indentured servants in the colonies distanced themselves little by little from blacks and demanded privileges that the law denied to slaves but granted to servants because of their European ancestry. Slaveholders and public officials favored the claims of white people, thereby widening the gap between slave and nonslave.

English arrogance soon found ways to rationalize the racist treatment of Native Americans and the enslavement of Africans, frequently by invoking the authority of biblical scripture. Whites, too, were divided by wealth, social class, and ethnic heritage. Nevertheless, they forged a common bond in their domination over blacks and Indians. Slaveholders measured social status from the numbers of slaves they owned or hired from other masters. Even poor whites, whether free or indentured, enjoyed the elevated status that came with the color of their skin.

Racism created great divisions in Chesapeake society. Imposed English customs were an affront to the belief systems of Native Americans. English attempts to force them to adopt the Christian religion, European consumer goods, English farming practices, and very different divisions of labor between men and women undermined traditional Indian ways of life. Native religious beliefs were strongly based on achieving harmony and balance between man and the natural world. Conflicts continued over land use and trade. The growing numbers of Africans eventually threatened the status of natives in colonial society. European notions of slavery were abhorrent to Indians. While some tribes tried to remain neutral on the issue in an effort to achieve peace with the English, others found subtle ways to express their displeasure with the practice.

Africans transported to Virginia and forced into an alien culture as adults had very different life experiences than did slave children born in the colonies. The two groups developed different strategies for survival. African-born slaves attached more importance to maintaining their traditional religions because much of their culture was tied to religious observance and ceremony. A Hausa proverb contains the prescription: "It is when one is in trouble that he remembers God." Although most Africans arrived in the Americas without possessions, they were not without memory and custom, for, as a Chagga proverb put it, "The head of a man is a hiding place, a receptacle." Creoles—American-born slaves—often made a creative mix of African and Anglo-American culture. Another Hausa maxim guided their strategy: "When the drumbeat changes, the dance changes."

Slavery also divided African-Americans into separate occupational and status groups that included foremen, drivers, gang leaders, field hands, tradesmen, and house servants. These were categories created by the slaveholders. Social hierarchies within a slave community were, like as not, based on a slave's personality or on the significance of his or her work to the community itself. The presence of free men and women of African heritage further complicated the picture. So did those with biracial parents. The lines drawn by a racially based slave system were blurry around the edges.

RACIAL SLAVERY CODIFIED

The institution of slavery was continually reshaped and redefined by government legislation and judgments of the court. The governor, Council, and House of Burgesses made laws setting the terms of slavery. Initially, punishments meted out to indentured servants and apprentices and laws regulating their behavior were extended to cover enslaved workers. Soon those laws proved to be inadequate. Workers held for life could not be required to compensate masters for infractions against the rules by extending their terms of service. Surprisingly quickly, from 1640 to 1662, slave owners interpreted customary law and enacted formal legislation to make lifelong servitude the common condition for all newly arrived Africans. Beginning in the 1660s, statutes also assigned the legal status of children born in Virginia according to the condition of the mother. Slave women had no legal protection against rape, and slave owners could hold in perpetual bondage any children they or other white men fathered with slave mothers.

The law became increasingly restrictive in the late seventeenth and early eighteenth centuries. It dictated a system of rigid social control: slaves were denied legal marriage, freedom of movement, and even the right to defend themselves against life-threatening physical abuse. A generation later, tutor Philip Vickers Fithian explained that "the slaves in this colony are never married, their lords thinking them improper subjects for so valuable an Institution." Other laws were passed in response to the growing fear of slave uprisings. Severe sentences could be handed out to slaves who stole white people's property, traveled without authorization, ran away, or resisted whipping or other punishments.

Virginia rulers sought to curb the growth of the free black population. The presence of free blacks challenged the legitimacy of the slave system. Legal grounds for manumission were narrowly defined until after the Revolution. Free blacks increasingly discovered that they were denied many of the rights accorded to free whites. They were not allowed to own guns, to hold indentured servants, to intermarry with whites, to bear witness against whites in court, or to hold offices of any kind. At the same time, they were obliged to pay higher taxes than comparable white families.

Courts' administration of the law further defined the terms of slavery. Justices of the peace applied a separate criminal code to cases involving blacks, used different trial procedures, and handed down harsher punishments. Notwithstanding, government officials and magistrates could provide redress for African-Virginians seeking mediation in disputes between masters and slaves and presenting petitions on a variety of issues. One-third of the petitions brought before the governor's Council between 1723 and 1775 were filed by slaves and free blacks. Matthew Ashby, a free black resident of Williamsburg, was one of the successful petitioners. After purchasing his wife and children from their owner, he asked the Council for permission to manumit them in November 1769. Ashby may also have joined a group of free blacks who asked the burgesses to repeal an unequal law requiring them to pay tithes on their wives and daughters over the age of sixteen. The burgesses granted their request in 1769. These petitioners cited ancient precedent for their tithe argument: Anthony Johnson, believed to have one of the earliest Africans to arrive in the colony in 1619, had sought the same consideration from a Virginia court in the 1640s, and he, too, had won his case.

Being enslaved meant always living in agonizing uncertainty. The only effective restraint on owners' total power over their human property was self-

The slave quarter at Carter's Grove plantation.

interest. Sometimes passion or greed overruled humanitarian instincts. Masters frequently and arbitrarily revoked long-standing privileges and protections established by informal custom. They could rape or maim their slaves with relative impunity. Courts seldom punished owners who killed slaves in a fit of passion or intoxication. Masters might break up slave families at any time through gift, sale, or hiring out, or force some to move to distant holdings far from their kin. Whenever a slave owner died or got into financial trouble, families were at risk of being parceled out among the owner's heirs and creditors with equally tragic results. These dangers separated slaves from other bonded laborers.

CRACKS IN THE SYSTEM

Educational institutions and the established church encouraged the acceptance and spread of slavery. Anglican ministers preached to black and white Virginians about their "God-given" roles in civilized society and enjoined slaves to accept their fate and obey their masters. The Bray School in Williamsburg taught young black children obedience along with the three R's. At home, white children learned to become masters and mistresses by watching their parents. Likewise, slave children learned survival strategies from their elders. Interestingly, African-Virginians bent both church and school to

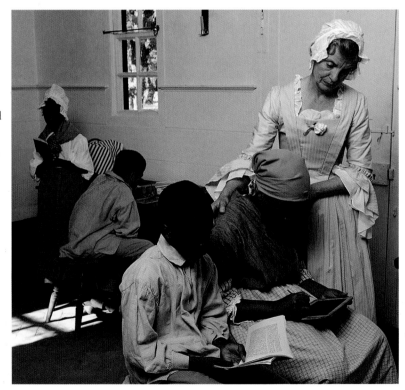

Black children learned to read and write at the Bray School in Williamsburg. They were also introduced to the catechism of the Church of England and taught behaviors suitable for African-Americans.

serve their own interests. Nearly one thousand slaves, children and adults, and a few free blacks were baptized at Bruton Parish Church between 1746 and 1768. Some hoped that accepting Christianity might lead to freedom; others may have sought special protection for their children. Blacks who learned to write in Williamsburg sometimes forged travel passes for other slaves, and readers discovered in the egalitarian pronouncements of white revolutionaries a powerful critique of their masters' hypocrisy.

One institution, the evangelical church, preached a different message. New Light Christians drew increasing numbers of slaves into their fold in the second half of the century by offering hope of deliverance from persecution. Many evangelicals and their followers openly denounced slavery. Some took their beliefs a step further by actively seeking its abolition. About the same time, black preachers began to form their own congregations and deliver openly antislavery messages. Biblical references to obedience were replaced with scriptural passages about the Israelites, Daniel and the Lion, and Job, which encouraged slaves to believe that freedom was possible in their lifetimes.

Against formidable odds, African-Virginians succeeded in establishing families, extending kin connections, and making friends with slaves at other plantations. Kinship networks and informal business relationships also included free blacks. The world blacks made for themselves helped to ease the isolation, loneliness, and degradation of slavery. Africans and their Virginia-born descendants developed their own system of social relations in the quarters. They developed a semiautonomous culture that borrowed from both African and English traditions. Observing customs that whites could not entirely control afforded slaves some small measure of power over their lives and nurtured their solidarity.

Little by little, and here and there, slaves' likes and dislikes worked significant changes in plantation routines, work assignments, and the operation of local exchange networks. By the early eighteenth century, for example, many slaves and masters had reached a general understanding about the minimum amounts of food, clothing, and shelter that owners were obliged to provide. In some cases, slaves were able to persuade owners to agree to "reasonable" hours of labor and levels of output. Slaves responded to arbitrary, unfavorable changes in plantation work rules with slowdowns and sabotage. Sometimes they feigned sickness or ran away. Artisans insisted on customary work routines and production requirements when masters tried to speed up work or to undercut their autonomy. By the 1770s, slaves and free blacks living in and around Williamsburg were active and knowledgeable participants in a local cash-based trading economy however much their actions were circumscribed. In theory, only chattels themselves, slaves gradually earned from grudging masters the "privilege" of keeping the profits from the produce they raised in their free time. They quickly transformed those limited privileges into more widely shared rights. By the end of the Revolutionary

War, many masters had come to accept their slaves' independent participation in local trading networks, however incongruent with the idea of slavery.

Masters had to concede that there were benefits to allowing slaves to own "property," a practice Thomas Jefferson called the "peculium." Owners recognized that the opportunity to own property got around one of the chief problems of slave labor: the lack of positive incentives. The practice of the peculium was widespread even if the term was not. Slave owners' wills and inventories from the Williamsburg vicinity rarely list clothing, utensils, poultry, or other livestock belonging to slaves. The omission was no oversight, but rather an acknowledgment of the fact that such things were the slaves' own possessions, not their masters'. Archaeological evidence makes it clear that slaves acquired a variety of goods. They purchased "luxury" items with the money they earned from their business ventures. Writing to Thomas Mann Randolph in 1798, Jefferson advised, "I thank you for putting an end to the cultivation of tobacco as the peculium of the negroes . . . I have ever found it necessary to confine them to such articles as are not raised on the farm. There is no other way of drawing a line between what is theirs & mine." Slaves throughout Virginia, particularly those who lived near urban areas, had many opportunities to buy, sell, and trade products and produce they made or grew themselves. Jefferson's concern about being unable to distinguish his property from that of his slaves shows just how lucrative slave enterprises could be.

THE STRAINED WORLD BLACKS AND WHITES MADE AND SHARED

Black and white cultures still retained distinctive traces of their English and African roots in mid-eighteenth-century Virginia. But both were also rapidly becoming hybrid cultures as interactions increased among Africans, Europeans, African-Virginians, and Anglo-Virginians. Blacks and whites were

Handkerchief, copper-plate printed linen, England, 1770–1785. Although printed in England, the handkerchief shows tobacco field laborers in Virginia.

Fashioned of clay from the Chesapeake region, the design on this pipe depicts ritual symbols used by some African peoples.

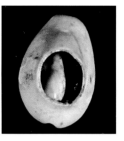

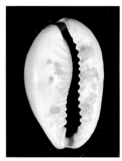

Cowrie shells were used in Africa as currency, for decoration, and in healing rituals. Their presence in the graves of African-Americans in Virginia suggests that the shells played a significant role in slave beliefs and ritual practices in the New World.

influencing each other's culture in their farming practices, use of medicine, building traditions, material culture, and art and music. The introduction of European stringed instruments expanded Africans' musical repertoire while at the same time slave musicians influenced the way European music was performed. Black musicians like Fiddler Billy of Williamsburg played at balls and other occasions. For their part, not a few Europeans found African instruments pleasing to the ear. European travelers frequently noted the popularity of "Negro jigs" among whites at the dances they attended in Virginia.

Musical traditions are relatively easy to identify. Africans' use and sometimes creative adaptation of European manufactured goods, while harder to document, provide further insights into the mixing of African and European cultures where they can be identified. Archaeological excavations reveal expensive ceramics and other personal items in storage pits at slave quarters. Slaves also made adaptive reuse of European religious beliefs. Blacks in large numbers embraced Christianity, especially during the Great Awakening, although they often introduced their own interpretations of scripture and their own versions of the liturgy.

Cultural sharing was not something that blacks or whites pursued deliberately. Yet the product of their interaction is evident everywhere historians look. Many blacks retained their West African religious belief in one supreme being. Africans and their descendants also believed in spirit possession, in the notion that God, or any of his designates, could physically possess the human body. Since evangelicals encouraged a more personal relationship with God, they were sympathetic to slaves' "fits of joy." Over time, this form of expression became common in both black and white evangelical denominations such as the Baptists and Methodists.

Understanding of the slave-master relationship has changed profoundly in recent years. Not only have scholars recognized cultural influences of blacks on whites, but closer examination reveals that slaves, too, exerted more of their influence in day-to-day interactions between the races than was previously supposed. In real life, the relationship between masters and slaves often contradicted law, custom, and prescribed status roles. For example, in 1778,

RUN-AWAY from the subscriber in *Norfolk*, about the 20th of *October* last, two young Negro fellows, *viz.* WILL, about 5 feet 8 inches high, middling black, well made, is an outlandish fellow, and when he is surprised the white of his eyes turns red; I bought him of Mr. *Moss*, about 8 miles below *York*, and imagine he is gone that way, or some where between *York* and *Williamsburg*. PETER, about 5 feet 9 inches high, a very black slim fellow, has a wife at *Little Town*, and a father at Mr. *Philip Burt's* quarter, near the half-way house between *Williamsburg* and *York*; he formerly belonged to Parson *Fontaine*, and I bought him of Doctor *James Carter*. They are both outlawed; and TEN POUNDS a piece offered to any person that will kill the said Negroes, and bring me their heads, or THIRTY SHILLINGS for each if brought home alive.
JOHN BROWN.

Legally, slaves were property. Their masters had the right to outlaw runaway slaves, thereby empowering free men to kill fugitives if they resisted arrest. This advertisement from the *Virginia Gazette* suggests that Will was likely running away and that he was worth more dead than alive to his master.

Anne Drummond of Williamsburg discovered that her house had been robbed. She accused her slave Sam of the crime. As punishment, she sold him to a plantation owner in Albemarle County. Sam was the only son of the Drummonds' cook and laundress, who simply refused to work after he was sold. For the next two years, the cook-laundress complained of a sore leg to avoid working for Mrs. Drummond while taking on paid tasks for others in the neighborhood. Anne Drummond finally relented in 1780. Deciding she might have judged Sam wrongly, Anne attempted to reunite mother and son.

Other slave families were not as fortunate. After obtaining freedom in Philadelphia in 1807, James Carter of Caroline County wrote, "My mother has had 9 Children and altho She and Mrs Armistead has been brought up together from little Girls, She has sufferd all my mothers Children to be picked from her. My mothers Family has Served the Family of Mrs Armistead upwards of one Hundred and 30 years."

At times, blacks and whites often formed emotional attachments to one another. Landon Carter's diary provides numerous insights into these peculiar friendships. His long and intimate relationships with different slaves on his property illustrate how attached Carter was to them, and how much he understood himself in terms of his relationship toward them. Carter considered himself the father to all on his property. He saw to his slaves' physical and medical needs and engaged in a variety of amusements with them, yet he could not understand why his "kindness" was not reciprocated with loyalty and honesty. His greatest companion appears to have been Nassau, who repeatedly ran away, cursed him, drank excessively, and even pilfered things from him. Carter punished Nassau and threatened to sell him, but invariably he ended up forgiving every transgression.

Sometimes masters actually sympathized with the plight of their slaves.

In 1787, Henry St. George Tucker took a slave boy named Bob with him to Winchester where he intended to practice law. The uprooted Bob became despondent beyond anything young Tucker had witnessed: "I enclose a short note from Bob to his mother. Poor little fellow! I was much affected at an incident last night. I was waked from a very sound sleep by a most piteous lamentation. I found it was Bob. 'What's the matter Bob?' 'I was dreaming about my mammy Sir!!!' cried he in melancholy distress. 'Gracious God!' thought I, how ought not I feel, who regarded this child an insensible when compared to those of our complexion. In truth our thoughts had been straying the same way. How finely woven, how delicately sensible must be those bonds of natural affection which equally adorn the civilized and the savage. The American and African—nay the man and the brute! I declare I know not a situation in which I have been lately placed that touched me so nearly as that incident I have just related." Despite his emotional bond with Bob, Tucker continued to use terms like "savage" and "brute" when referring to blacks.

Perhaps the least discussed yet most enduring consequence of the interactions between blacks and whites is miscegenation. Interracial sex and procreation between Africans and Europeans began almost from the first contact in Africa and the Americas. The 1662 law that defined a child's status based on the status of the mother passed on lifelong servitude to children born of mixed parents. Another law made it illegal for "any Christian to fornicate with a Negro man or woman." Offenders were required to pay double the fine assessed on unmarried couples of European origin. *Mulattoes,* a term applied to children born of African and European parents, is found in practically every slave inventory, runaway ad, law regarding slaves, and planter diary. Unlike the Spaniards or Portuguese, the English did not differentiate between those who were one-half, one-quarter, or less black or white. Mulatto was used for any person of mixed parentage. Black women were not the only females who had mulatto children. Native American and white women also gave birth to children of mixed race. A law enacted four separate times—in 1691, 1705, 1753, and 1765—stipulated that "women servants or free Christian white women servants who have a bastard child by a negro or mulatto" must pay a fine, serve an additional term of service, and have the child bound out to the parish. Quite a few free blacks born of Englishwomen gained their freedom from their mothers. Determining the numbers and types of mulatto births in Virginia is difficult without further research. How such children and their parents were treated by blacks and whites continues to be a topic of speculation.

Many encounters between blacks and whites were violent. Fithian recounted an incident near Nomini Hall involving a boastful overseer who described his remedy for slaves who were sullen, obstinate, or idle. The tutor wrote, "Says he, Take a Negro, strip him, tie him fast to a post; take then a sharp Curry-Comb, & curry him severely til he is well scraped; & call a Boy with some dry hay, and make the Boy rub him down for several minutes, then salt him, & unlose him. He will attend to his Business."

Such acts of depravity against slaves were common. Occasionally, the victims retaliated. John Greenhow placed an ad in the *Virginia Gazette* on January 17, 1777: "Run away from the subscriber, in Williamsburg, the two following men, viz. Fox, about 40 years old, who is clad in cotton, and about ten days ago beat his overseer and went off. Emanuel, upwards of six feet high, about 26 years old, a strong able fellow, of a daring resolute temper, very subtle [illeg.] John Greenhow."

Arson and robbery appear to have been the two most common forms of retaliation by slaves. After James Hubbard's house was set on fire in January 1770, two slaves were charged with the crime. Isaac, who belonged to Katherine Hubbard, received the death sentence. Hubbard's slave David was charged with "instigating and abetting." The court found David innocent but jailed him as a "dangerous person." Courts seldom prosecuted masters for violence against or murder of slaves, especially if the act was the result of correction. The law required testimony from "one lawful and credible witness." Slaves, the most likely witnesses, could not testify against their masters or, for that matter, any other whites.

An Overseer Doing His Duty, by Benjamin Latrobe, watercolor on paper, near Fredericksburg, Va., March 13, 1798. Courtesy, Maryland Historical Society, Baltimore, Md. Overseers supervised slaves working in tobacco fields.

A SCHEME of a LOTTERY

For difpofing of certain LANDS, SLAVES, and STOCKS, belonging to the fubfcriber.

CONTENTS of PRIZES.

Priz.		Value.	
1 of		£. 5000	TO confift of a forge and geared grift-mill, both well fixed, and fituate on a plentiful and conftant ftream, with 1800 acres of good land, in King and Queen county, near Todd's Bridge; which coft 6000l.
1 of		1375	To confift of 550 acres of very good land, lying in King William county, on Pamunkey river, called Gooch's, part of 1686 acres, purchafed of William Claiborne, deceafed; the line to extend from faid river to the back line acrofs towards Mattapony.
1 of		1925	To confift 550 acres of very good land, adjoining and below the faid tract lying on Pamunkey river, whereon is a good dwelling-houfe, 70 feet long and 20 feet wide, with three rooms below and three above; alfo all other good and convenient out-houfes; 1000 fine peach trees thereon, with many apple trees and other forts of fruit, a fine high and pleafant fituation, and the plantation in exceeding good order for cropping; the line to extend from faid river to the back line towards Mattapony.
1 of		1750	To confift of 586 acres, below the aforefaid two tracts; whereon is a fine peach orchard, and many fine apple trees; the plantation is in exceeding good order for cropping, and very fine for corn and tobacco, and abounds with a great quantity of white oak, which will afford, it's thought, a thoufand pounds worth of plank and ftaves.
65 of	£. 50	3250	To confift of 6500 acres of good land, in Caroline county; to be laid off in lots of 100 acres each.
4 of	75	300	To confift of 812 acres of good land, in Spotfylvania county, in the fork between Northanna and the North Fork, with a large quantity of low grounds, and meadow land; to be laid off in lots of 203 acres each.
1 of		180	A Negro man named Billy, about 22 years old, an exceeding trufty good forgeman, as well at the finery as under the hammer, and underftands putting up his fire; Alfo his wife named Lucy, a young wench, who works exceeding well both in the houfe and field.
1 of		200	A Negro man named Joe, about 27 years old, a very trufty good forgeman, as well at the finery as under the hammer, and underftands putting up his fire.
1 of		200	A Negro man named Mingo, about 24 years old, a very trufty good finer, and hammerman, and underftands putting up his fire.
1 of		180	A Negro man named Ralph, about 22 years old, an exceeding good finer.
1 of		120	A Negro man named Ifaac, about 20 years old, an exceeding good hammerman and finer.
1 of		250	A Negro man named Sam, about 26 years old, a fine chaferyman; alfo his wife Daphne, a very good hand at the hoe, or in the houfe.
1 of		200	A Negro man named Abraham, about 26 years old, an exceeding good forge carpenter, cooper, and clapboard carpenter.
1 of		150	A Negro man named Bob, about 27 years old, a very fine mafter collier.
1 of		90	A Negro man named Dublin, about 30 years old, a very good collier.
1 of		90	A Negro man named London, about 25 years old, a very good collier.
1 of		90	A Negro man named Cambridge, about 24 years old, a good collier.
1 of		90	A Negro man named Harry, a very good collier.
1 of		100	A Negro man named Toby, a very fine mafter collier.
1 of		120	A Negro man named Peter, about 18 years old, an exceeding trufty good waggoner.
1 of		190	A Negro man named Dick, about 24 years old, a very fine blackfmith; alfo his fmith's tools.
1 of		80	A Negro man named Sampfon, about 32 years old, the Skipper of the flat.
1 of		70	A Negro man named Dundee, about 38 years old, a good planter.
1 of		85	A Negro man named Caroline Joe, about 35 years old, a very fine planter.
1 of		110	A Negro woman named Rachel, about 32 years old, and her children Daniel and Thompfon, both very fine.
1 of		70	A Negro woman named Hannah, about 16 years old.
1 of		75	A Negro man named Jack, a good planter.
1 of		75	A Negro man named Ben, about 25 years old, a good houfe fervant, and a good carter, &c.
1 of		120	A Negro man, Robin, a good fawyer, and Bella, his wife.
1 of		70	A Negro girl named Sukey, about 12 years old, and another named Betty, about 7 years old; children of Robin and Bella.
1 of		75	A Negro man named York, a good fawyer.
1 of		80	A Negro woman named Kate, and a young child, Judy.
1 of		60	A Negro girl, Aggy, and boy, Nat; children of Kate.
1 of		75	A Negro named Pompey, a young fellow.
1 of		110	A fine breeding woman named Pat, lame of one fide, with child, and her three children, Lett, Milley, and Charlotte.
1 of		60	A fine boy, Phill, fon of Patty, about 14 years old.
1 of		50	A Negro man named Tom, an outlandifh fellow.
1 of		280	A Negro man named Cæfar about 30 years old, a very good blackfmith; and his wife named Nanny, with two children, Tab and Jane.
1 of		110	A Negro man named Edom, about 23 years old, a blackfmith who has ferved four years to the trade.
1 of		160	A Negro man named Mofes, about 23 years old, a very good planter, and his wife Phœbe, a fine young wench, with her child Nell.
1 of		50	A Negro woman, Dorah, wife of carpenter Jemmy.
1 of		35	A Negro named Venus, daughter of Tab.
1 of		25	A Negro named Judy, wife of Sambo.
1 of		20	A Negro named Lucy, outlandifh.
1 of		25	A Negro man named Toby, a good miller.
1 of		100	A team of exceeding fine horfes, confifting of four, and their gear; alfo a good waggon.
1 of		80	A team of four horfes, and their gear, with two coal waggons.
10 of	20	200	To confift of 100 head of cattle, to be laid off in 10 lots.

124 PRIZES £. 18,400
1716 BLANKS

1840 TICKETS at 10l. each, Is £. 18,400.

Managers are JOHN RANDOLPH, JOHN BAYLOR, GEORGE WASHINGTON, FIELDING LEWIS, ARCHIBALD CARY, CARTER BRAXTON, BENJAMIN HARRISON, RALPH WORMLEY, RICHARD HENRY LEE, THOMAS WALKER, THOMAS TABB, EDMUND PENDLETON, PETER LYONS, PATRICK COUTTS, NEIL JAMIESON, ALEXANDER DONALD, DAVID JAMESON, and JOHN MADISON, Gentlemen.

Contrary to my expectation, the drawing of the above LOTTERY is obliged to be deferred for a fhort time.

N. B. Not any of the cattle mentioned in this lottery, are to be under the age of two years, nor none to exceed 4 or five years old.

tt

BERNARD MOORE.

MIDDLESEX, November 15, 1768.

THIS is to give notice to all adventurers in my lottery, that it will certainly be drawn on the third Friday in December, at Mr. George Channing's ordinary, in Middlefex county. All that bought tickets are defired to meet me there and pay the money, and receive their prizes (if fortunate) or fend a perfon to act for them, as no further care will be take of the prizes after that day, and hope none will expect any indulgence, as the price of a ticket is fo trifling. Their compliance will greatly oblige Their moft obedient and very humble fervant, SAMUEL DANIEL.

NORFOLK, October 30, 1768.

Juft imported in the Bowman, Capt. Stevenfon, from Glafgow, and the Jordan, Capt. Woodford, from London, and to be fold cheap, for ready money or fhort credit, by the fubfcribers at their ftore near the Market Houfe, Norfolk,

A LARGE and complete affortment of EUROPEAN and EAST INDIA GOODS. Likewife good Weft-India RUM, SUGAR, and MOLASSES.
t.f.   LOGAN, GILMOUR, & Co.

Feb. 10, 1768.
To be SOLD at private SALE,

SIX THOUSAND FIVE HUNDRED ACRES of LAND, pleafantly fituate on James river; 4 acres of land, with a water grift mill, on Mayfer's creek, in the fame county; and two thoufand acres of land in Halifax county; they will be fold altogether, or divided into lots, as may beft fuit the purchafers. Thefe lands were the eftate of Mr. William Kennon, and are conveyed to us (with others his truftees) for the benefit of his creditors. As a fale of thefe lands has been before advertifed, but not effected; it may not be improper, to affure the public, that an abfolute difpofal of them is now intended; and that we fhall be ready at all times to receive propofals for the whole, or any part thereof. Mr. John Chriftian (who lives thereon) will fhew the land in Charles City.
RICHARD RANDOLPH,
JAMES BELSCHES,
JERMAN BAKER.

TO BE SOLD,

UPWARDS of ONE THOUSAND ACRES of LAND, near the Double Top Mountain in Culpeper county, late the property of Mr. John Rootes in Gloucefter county. Any perfon inclinable to purchafe, may apply to Mr. Roger Dixon, in Fredericksburg, who is impowered to agree. The land will be laid off in lots if defired.

RICHMOND county, July 14.

RUN away about the 20th of May laft, an Eaft-India Indian, named Thomas Greenwich; he is a well made fellow, about 5 feet 4 inches high, wears his own hair, which is long and black, has a thin vifage, a very fly look, and a remarkable fet of fine white teeth. A reward of 40s. will be paid the perfon who delivers him to the fubfcriber, befides what the law allows.   WILLIAM COLSTON.

October 2, 1768.

STRAYED or ftolen from King William court-houfe, about fix weeks ago, a bay horfe, about 14 hands high, with a black mane and tail, branded on the nigh fhoulder I: on the nigh buttock W: paces, trots, and gallops, and draws very well in a chair. Whoever will bring the faid horfe to Mr. Holt Richefon, or fecure him fo as I may get him again, fhall receive TWENTY SHILLINGS reward. ALEX: GLASS STRACHAN.

SCHEME of a LOTTERY

FOR difpofing of one hundred and forty-fix LOTS of LAND, in the town of Hanover, yet remaining unfold. The leaft valuable of the lots, according to the prices of thofe moft remote from the river, which have been fold, not being lefs than £. 20, which is far below what was given for feveral near the river.

	lots	value	rent.
Infpection at Page's, 5 lots, at 12 years purchafe,		£. 840	£. 70
Do. Crutchfield's, 6 lots at do.		720	60
		2560	230
Lots improved, each half acre, at £. 20	135	2700	230
		4260	230
137 Prizes.	137		
263 Blanks.			
400 Tickets at £. 10 each,		4000	

The faid lottery will be drawn at Mr. Anthony Hay's in Williamfburg, as foon as the tickets are difpofed of. Thofe who do not pay or their tickets on the day of drawing, may give bond to carry intereft from that time. Robert Carter Nicolas, George Wythe, Thomas Everard, John Thompfon, and Jerman Baker, Efqrs; managers, or any three, of whom tickets may be had, and of the fubfcriber.

MANN PAGE.

Slaves were sold as property along with land, equipment, and livestock in a lottery advertisement from the *Virginia Gazette*.

CONCLUSION

The unwillingness of whites to recognize the full and equal humanity of blacks led to many injustices and inhumanities. By the end of the eighteenth century, slavery was no longer just an economic and "necessary evil." It had become a way of life. Whites were enslaved to the myth of their own superiority while blacks bore the burden of slavery's terrible reality. Racism, taking root in the slave system, sowed the seeds of future discord, injustice, injury, and emotional desolation.

Despite legislative decrees reinforcing the slave system, whites grew increasingly fearful as the number of blacks increased. That fear fueled repression and violence. Governments guaranteed white Virginians the right to coerce their human property, but realities of everyday management undermined those guarantees. Many whites believed that people held against their will, if not strictly controlled, might seek to throw off the bonds of servitude by force and harm the individuals responsible for their enslavement.

The specter of insurrection excited the greatest fear of all. Jefferson wrote, "Deep rooted prejudices entertained by whites; ten thousand recollections by the blacks, of the injuries they have sustained; new provocations; . . . will divide us into parties, and produce convulsions which will probably never end but in the extermination of the one or the other race." Jefferson recognized that slavery could no longer be justified: "Indeed I tremble for my country, when I reflect that God is just: that his justice cannot sleep forever: . . . The Almighty has no attribute which can side with us in such a contest." He was unable to resolve the issue in his private or public life. He found no answers that would at once satisfy his conscience and his finances. Like many of his contemporaries, Jefferson chose to let the next generation discover the answers to the problem of race and slavery in American society.

"ENSLAVING VIRGINIA" AND THE "BECOMING AMERICANS" THEME

DIVERSE PEOPLE

By the time the English settled Virginia, the practice of enslaving Africans and transporting them to the Americas had already been a well-established trade for almost 150 years in the Portuguese and Spanish colonies in the New World. Slavery took many forms in Africa, all of them different from the ways it developed in the Western Hemisphere under the influence of colonization. The institution acquired still other characteristics and practices in British North America.

CLASHING INTERESTS

Enslaving Virginia's black population provided the central dynamic in the development of a distinctive Virginia culture. Slavery gave new definition to European notions of a structured society with the landed aristocracy on top and merchant and working classes below. The slave system made a more basic distinction. It divided social groups into free and unfree. Slavery reinforced Anglo-Virginians' Eurocentric views of racial and ethnic superiority.

SHARED VALUES

Inherent in the term *accommodation* is the idea of acceptance. But, since slaves had no access to justice or redress through the legal system, accommodation must be understood in strictly personal terms. Any latitude given to a slave usually violated statute law. Yet masters and slaves were often willing to live with these contradictions so long as the concessions struck a balance between the slave's concern for family and a modicum of freedom, and the master's concern for control and a margin of profitability.

FORMATIVE INSTITUTIONS

As increasing numbers of Africans were imported into Virginia, laws regarding their status, racial distinction, and freedom of movement developed apace. With each passing generation, social and civic institutions (churches, schools, law courts, and governments) reinforced conditions of servitude and reshaped the role of Africans in Virginia society. Although freeing slaves became easier during the revolutionary era, punishments for even small infractions of the law became ever more severe and inhumane.

PARTIAL FREEDOMS

White Virginians regarded the ownership of other humans as their prerogative and justified it on the grounds of racial superiority. Black Virginians were left to make do. They sought any way possible to maintain family life and whatever freedoms they could beg, borrow, or steal from their masters. Blacks and whites learned how to "play by the rules" even if the rules were exceptions to the rule.

REVOLUTIONARY PROMISE

The institution of slavery established an unresolvable, inherent contradiction in Virginia culture that transcended even the white man's self-serving justification. As Virginians imposed a slave system on an entire race of individuals, their actions inevitably defined their relationship to Great Britain as one between masters and slaves. The failure of southern colonists to extend their revolutionary rhetoric to slaves led to petitions and increasing numbers of runaways. Virginians allowed economic interests to cloud their moral judgment.

Connections to Other "Becoming Americans" Story Lines

Just as the institution of slavery cut across every aspect of society in eighteenth-century Virginia, it runs through the interpretation of every "Becoming Americans" story line at Colonial Williamsburg.

Taking Possession

The success of Virginia's tobacco economy fueled the desire for the continued expansion and development of Virginia's natural resources. African-Virginians' labor provided much of the manpower for extending settlement and increasing the wealth of slave owners. The concept of private landowning was at first incomprehensible to Africans. They came from societies with a tradition of corporate landholding, as was also the case among Native Americans. Soon after Africans began arriving in the Chesapeake, free Africans and African-Virginians recognized that the private land rights English settlers valued afforded advantages such as enhanced social status, greater family security, and a measure of independence. But whites did not permit slaves to participate in the settlement process except for the labor they contributed. However, beneath the ordered landscape that freeholding Virginians created, African-Virginians imposed a far different structure on the land. On the quarters they occupied, they reinstituted communal land use practices such as the notion that everyone who worked the land should reap an equal share of its fruits.

Redefining Family

The presence of Africans profoundly affected the evolution of family life in Virginia. White households included slaves as members of their extended families. African-Virginians developed their own nuclear and extended families within the confines of the slave system. Even when disrupted by sales or the practice of hiring out, the black family maintained kinship networks essential for strong family ties.

Buying Respectability

In Virginia, slaves were a commodity just like other goods. The wealth and status of white Virginians were defined in part by the number of humans they owned. Although in theory slaves could not be property holders, they began to participate in Virginia's consumer culture during the second half of the eighteenth century. Merchants willingly accepted the cash that slaves earned from selling produce or by working in their limited free time in exchange for goods they wanted to buy. Although social respectability remained elusive, slaves participated in the economy because it afforded a degree of autonomy and a few comforts.

CHOOSING REVOLUTION

Property rights lay at the heart of the choice many Virginians eventually made in favor of independence from Great Britain. Slaves represented significant property holdings that white Virginians fought to preserve. Ironically, revolutionary leaders used the terms *liberty* and *slavery* to defend their property and to advance their political rights. To them, slavery meant loss of freedom under the tyranny of British misrule. To Virginia's 200,000 slaves, the words defined their condition in the most personal sense. Hundreds risked their lives by responding to Lord Dunmore's November 1775 proclamation offering freedom to slaves and indentured servants who rallied to his side. Alternatively, some free blacks chose to enlist in the American army or navy. Most of the African-Americans who labored actively for the patriot cause did so involuntarily, however. The Virginia government rented slaves as wagoners, miners, pilots, hospital attendants, and common laborers. Less often, they were hired as soldiers to substitute for free men. The government bought others outright. Although a few gained freedom as a result of their service, most returned to slavery after the war.

FREEING RELIGION

Africans brought to Virginia a variety of religious beliefs and practices. As the slave population increased, their native religions became creolized. By the mid-eighteenth century, only a few elements persisted—particularly the idea of spirit possession. When evangelical Christians began to accept blacks into their congregations, worship services changed to reflect the inclusion of Africans. Several evangelical denominations even began to recognize and eventually to ordain black preachers.

Story Line Team: Christy Matthews, Anne Willis, Ywone Edwards, Carson Hudson, Martha Katz-Hyman, Ann Parker, Julie Richter, Marcel Riddick, and Lorena Walsh.

FURTHER READING

Berlin, Ira. *Many Thousands Gone: The First Two Centuries of Slavery in North America.* Cambridge, Mass.: Belknap Press of Harvard University Press, 1998.

Curtin, Philip D., ed. *Africa Remembered: Narratives by West Africans from the Era of the Slave Trade.* Madison, Wis.: University of Wisconsin Press, 1967.

Dunn, Richard S. "Black Society in the Chesapeake, 1776–1810." In *Slavery and Freedom in the Age of the American Revolution.* Edited by Ira Berlin and Ronald Hoffman, pp. 49–82. Charlottesville, Va.: University Press of Virginia, 1983.

Ferguson, Leland. *Uncommon Ground: Archaeology and Early African America, 1650–1800.* Washington, D. C.: Smithsonian Institution Press, 1992.

Frey, Sylvia R. *Water from the Rock: Black Resistance in a Revolutionary Age.* Princeton, N. J.: Princeton University Press, 1991.

Gundersen, Joan Rezner. "The Double Bonds of Race and Sex: Black and White Women in a Colonial Virginia Parish." *Journal of Southern History,* LII (1986), pp. 351–372.

Hughes, Sarah S. "Slaves for Hire: The Allocation of Black Labor in Elizabeth City County, Virginia, 1782 to 1810." *William and Mary Quarterly,* 3rd Ser., XXXV (1978), pp. 260–286.

Jordan, Winthrop D. *White Over Black: American Attitudes Toward the Negro, 1550–1812.* Chapel Hill, N. C.: University of North Carolina Press, 1968.

Katz-Hyman, Martha B. "'In the Middle of this Poverty Some Cups and a Teapot': The Furnishing of Slave Quarters at Colonial Williamsburg." In *The American Home: Material Culture, Domestic Space, and Family Life.* Edited by Eleanor McD. Thompson. Wintherthur, Del.: Henry Francis du Pont Wintherthur Museum, 1998.

Klein, Herbert S. *The Atlantic Slave Trade.* Cambridge: Cambridge University Press, 1999.

Kulikoff, Allen. "A 'Prolifick' People: Black Population Growth in the Chesapeake Colonies, 1700–1790." *Southern Studies,* XVI (1977), pp. 391–428.

_____. *Tobacco and Slaves: The Development of Southern Cultures in the Chesapeake, 1680–1800.* Chapel Hill, N. C.: University of North Carolina Press, 1986.

Lee, Jean Butenhoff. "The Problem of Slave Community in the Eighteenth-Century Chesapeake." *William and Mary Quarterly,* 3rd Ser., XLIII (1986), pp. 333–361.

McColley, Robert. *Slavery and Jeffersonian Virginia.* Urbana, Ill.: University of Illinois Press, 1964.

Menard, Russell R. "From Servants to Slaves: The Transformation of the Chesapeake Labor System." *Southern Studies,* XVI (1977), pp. 355–390.

_____. "The Maryland Slave Population, 1658 to 1730: A Demographic Profile of Blacks in Four Counties." *William and Mary Quarterly,* 3rd. Ser., XXXII (1975), pp. 29–54.

Morgan, Edmund S. *American Slavery, American Freedom: The Ordeal of Colonial Virginia.* New York: W. W. Norton, 1975.

Morgan, Philip D. *Slave Counterpoint: Black Culture in the Eighteenth-Century Chesapeake and Lowcountry.* Chapel Hill, N. C.: University of North Carolina Press, 1998.

Schwarz, Philip J. *Twice Condemned: Slaves and the Criminal Laws of Virginia, 1705–1865.* Baton Rouge, La.: Louisiana State University Press, 1988.

Shammas, Carole. "Black Women's Work and the Evolution of Plantation Society in Virginia." *Labor History,* XXVI (1985), pp. 5–28.

Singleton, Theresa A. "The Archaeology of Slave Life." In *Before Freedom Came: African-American Life in the Antebellum South.* Edited by Edward D. C. Campbell, Jr., with Kym Rice. Published for the Museum of the Confederacy, Richmond, Va. Charlottesville, Va.: University Press of Virginia, 1991.

Sobel, Mechal. *The World They Made Together: Black and White Values in Eighteenth-Century Virginia.* Princeton, N. J.: Princeton University Press, 1987.

Tate, Thad W. *The Negro in Eighteenth-Century Williamsburg.* Williamsburg, Va.: Colonial Williamsburg Foundation, 1965.

Thornton, John. *Africa and Africans in the Making of the Atlantic World, 1400–1680.* Cambridge: Cambridge University Press, 1992.

Vaughan, Alden T. "The Origins Debate: Slavery and Racism in Seventeenth-Century Virginia." *Virginia Magazine of History and Biography,* XCVII (1989), pp. 311–354.

Walsh, Lorena S. *From Calabar to Carter's Grove: The History of a Virginia Slave Community.* Charlottesville, Va." University Press of Virginia, 1997.

————. "Slave Life, Slave Society, and Tobacco Production in the Tidewater Chesapeake." In *Cultivation and Culture: Labor and the Shaping of Slave Life in the Americas.* Edited by Ira Berlin and Philip D. Morgan, pp. 170–199. Charlottesville, Va.: University Press of Virginia, 1993.

Yentsch, Anne Elizabeth. *A Chesapeake Family and Their Slaves: A Study in Historical Archaeology.* Cambridge: Cambridge University Press, 1994.

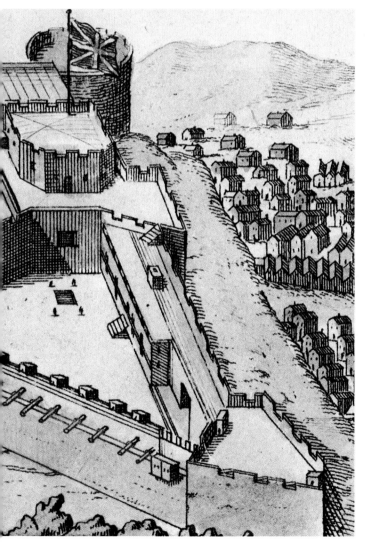

Detail of Cape Coast Castle, Guinea, from
Africa, by John Bowles, hand-colored engrav-
ing, London, ca. 1740. Many enslaved Africans
were shipped to the Western Hemisphere from
Cape Coast Castle, an English outpost on the
Gold Coast of West Africa.

Clothes make the man. Williamsburg milliners show a customer the newest styles from London.

BREWED BY **THE ST. GEORGE BREWING COMPANY**, HAMPTON, VIRGINIA, 23666. 5.0% ALCOHOL BY VOLUME. TO FIND OUT MORE ABOUT OUR BREWERY AND OUR FULL-BODIED BRITISH-STYLE ALES, VISIT US AT WWW.STGEORGEBREWINGCO.COM. INGREDIENTS: WATER, MALTED BARLEY, HOPS AND YEAST.

THE ST. GEORGE
BREWING COMPANY

INDIA
PALE ALE

AWARD WINNING CRAFT BREWED BRITISH STYLE ALES.

12 FLUID OUNCES

BUYING
RESPECTABILITY

Well-informed and highly skilled, tailors guided their clientele in making the right clothing choices.

BUYING
RESPECTABILITY

The "Buying Respectability" story line describes the "consumer revolution," the far-reaching transformation in people's standards and styles of living that revolutionized trade, commerce, technology, and, ultimately, the way people lived at every level of society. Seeking respectability, many people craved fashionable wardrobes, formal houses, the latest tablewares, and a variety of social refinements.

KEY POINTS

- BACKGROUND.   During the Middle Ages, everyday domestic life among all classes except the nobility required very little in the way of clothing, furniture, and food-related equipment. A person's reputation was measured by the amount of land, labor, and livestock he owned.

- RISING DEMAND.   By 1700, growing numbers of ordinary people in northern Europe and America began to demand and acquire newly available consumer goods, use services, and engage in social, recreational, and educational activities, all of which went far beyond meeting or improving their basic physical needs.

- CREATING AN IMAGE.   To achieve respectability within an increasingly urbane mobile society, affluent Virginians dressed in the latest London fashions and built houses suitable for entertaining. They furnished their houses with new furniture forms, took tea from the newest tea wares, and learned the rules of polished behavior that reaffirmed their position within their social station and differentiated them from the lower ranks.

- SELLING RESPECTABILITY.   By mid-century, local tradesmen and merchants offered an ever-increasing variety of consumer goods and services made possible by advances in British business practices and industrial technology.

- DEMOCRATIZATION.   Widespread possession of fashionable items, combined with etiquette-book manners, contributed to a novel idea—equality—a belief in every person's equal worth and his or her right to strive for a better life.

- CLASHING INTERESTS.   The consumer revolution was rejected by some, disadvantaged others, and led to a variety of conflicts. The tug-of-war between haves and have-nots, slave and free, men and women, country and city, and different religious groups became ever more apparent over time.

- COMING OF THE REVOLUTION.   Their widely shared democratic experience as consumers enabled Americans of various backgrounds to express in unison their anger at Parliament and their resolve to oppose what they perceived as its unjust laws.

BACKGROUND AND THESIS

Enter the hall of a medieval house in the English countryside. It is home to a prosperous landowner and his family, but amenities seem few and far between. There is no chimney, so smoke from the massive central hearth lingers in the air before reaching the high rafters. Big pots for boiling soups and stews, the typical meals, hang over the fire. The multipurpose room is quite dark since there are few windows. Peering through the gloom, we see that the hall, though large, contains almost no furniture. A woven or painted wall hanging covers one of the plastered walls. At mealtimes, tables—nothing more than boards laid over trestles—are set in place and covered with a rug or linen cloth. Backless benches seat the diners, and one or two cupboards stand against the walls. Silver cups and platters are stored away under lock and key because such precious items are displayed only when visitors are present to admire them. Diners scoop up the stew with spoons and fingers from com-

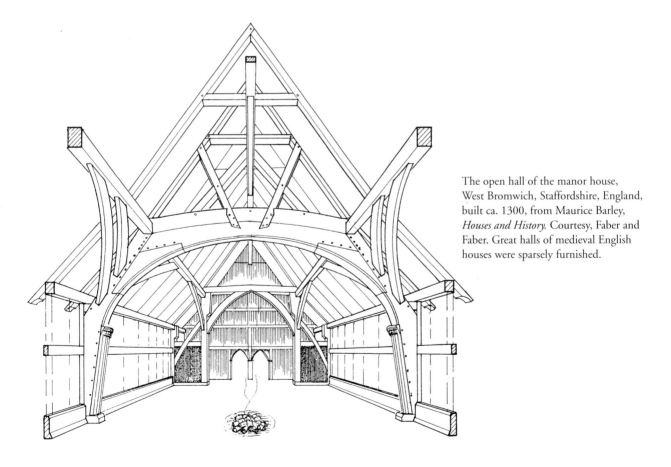

The open hall of the manor house, West Bromwich, Staffordshire, England, built ca. 1300, from Maurice Barley, *Houses and History.* Courtesy, Faber and Faber. Great halls of medieval English houses were sparsely furnished.

munal vessels and spear pieces of meat on the point of a knife. The master and mistress sleep in an upstairs chamber in the best bed in the house, which is covered and maybe curtained with costly textiles for privacy and warmth. They own relatively few articles of clothing and a piece or two of jewelry.

Before the seventeenth century, being rich meant having more but not living all that differently from one's poorer neighbors. Prosperous Britons acquired more household goods and personal possessions, but most objects met basic needs: bedding, a bedstead, and additional cooking equipment to prepare a wider range of foods. A man's reputation was a matter of common knowledge in medieval times. His neighbors measured his worth by the amount of land, labor, and livestock he owned or commanded, not by the cut of his coat or the fashion of his table.

Generations later in colonial Virginia's small capital city, the standard of living of Betty and Peyton Randolph is markedly different. They occupy a handsome frame house with glazed sash windows. Four principal rooms upstairs and four down are special-purpose spaces for entertaining family and a select group of friends. They own all the right equipment to engage in a variety of genteel activities—witness their parlor with a dozen mahogany chairs, a looking glass, a card table, two tea tables, sets of china, and a fine Wilton carpet on the floor. Across the wide central passage in a newly constructed wing is the dining room reserved for formal meals. Another carpet covers this floor. Two tables and twelve chairs, all made of imported mahogany, stand along the walls ready to be arranged as the occasion requires. A fashionable bowfat holds specialized dinnerware—dozens of china plates, china bowls, and china mugs, wineglasses, beer glasses, punch glasses, water glasses, silver knives and forks, and coffee cups and saucers. Service is an important part of the Randolphs' dining practice, as articles such as the sideboard table, soup tureen, sauceboats, tray, decanters, six japanned waiters, and the tea board attest.

Peyton Randolph's household inventory, January 5, 1776. York County, Va., Records, Wills and Inventories, 22. Courtesy, Circuit Court of York County, Yorktown, Va. Randolph's inventory shows that his parlor and dining room contained many special-use objects.

The changes in the way people lived from the Middle Ages to the period we interpret at Colonial Williamsburg is almost unimaginable to modern, comfort-loving visitors. What caused the drastic change in lifestyles and so greatly improved standards of living? Many factors combined to make new consumer goods available to nearly everyone in the late seventeenth and eighteenth centuries. Incomes were rising, so more people had more money left after they acquired the bare necessities. Although historians are still struggling to define the relationship between supply and demand, it is clear that mechanization, the factory system, faster, cheaper transportation, and the Industrial Revolution were preceded by the phenomenon we now call the "consumer revolution." The term refers to the total revision of expectations. In the eighteenth century, more and more people in Europe and the colonies desired goods and services that would have been unimaginable a few decades before.

Why this new demand? As society became more mobile, social rank was no longer communicated by houses, land, and livestock alone. By the late seventeenth century, ordinary men and women began to demand consumer goods that indicated their status. Consumption and display went well beyond basic human needs for a warm place to sleep and food on the table. People wanted fashionable, portable, status-bearing goods. Embroidered waistcoats, card tables, sets of carved chairs, and services of china plates and silver forks communicated their owners' rising standard of living and their style and worth.

Items that once were considered luxuries reserved for the ruling class began to "trickle down" to common households in the late seventeenth and eighteenth centuries. As a result, owning such things no longer elevated the well-to-do above their inferiors. The elite responded by seeking new status symbols to differentiate them from the clamoring horde. The middling and poorer sorts—and occasionally even slaves—kept up as best they could.

Each group sought to stay ahead of the folks below, so the wheel of changing fashion turned faster and faster. Gradually, as the latest commodities became more plentiful and affordable, traditional regional folkways were forced to compete with the new internationally recognized store-bought culture. The increasingly frantic pace of change and the widening range of people caught up in it propelled the consumer revolution.

One way the gentry set themselves apart was by cultivating social skills and engaging in leisure activities that working people had no time to learn or practice. Accomplished dancing, games of skill, tea drinking, and fine dining expressed their sophistication. Using their leisure time for intellectual pursuits in literature, natural science, and other subjects, the gentry aspired to the true refinement of both their inner and outer selves. With the growing importance of these civilities came the need for *even more* brand-new goods and services. The newest, often exclusive luxuries introduced at mid-century sym-

Frances Carter, by John Wollaston, Sr., oil on canvas, probably Virginia, 1750–1760. Every inch the gentry lady!

bolized all the appearances and dimensions that separated the highest rank of society from all others.

The debate continues about exactly when and why demand began, but it is clear that these unprecedented changes in how people lived could never have occurred without the ever-increasing availability of consumer goods. The "Buying Respectability" story line explores both the reasons for the consumer revolution and how the insatiable demand for new goods and services was met.

Family Group, by Charles Phillips, oil on canvas, London, ca. 1730. This family group epitomizes gentility as they enjoy refined conversation, music, and dance.

The Dinner. Symptoms of Eating and Drinking, engraved by W. Dickinson after a drawing by Henry Bunbury, colored stipple engraving, probably London, 1794.

CREATING ONE'S OWN IMAGE

The consumer revolution that began in northern Europe soon spread to the New World. Americans in particular quickly earned a reputation for their enthusiasm for material things. "Pride of wealth is as ostentatious in this country as ever the pride of birth has been elsewhere," an English traveler declared. Other commentators despaired that consumer extravagance had reached new extremes in the colonies.

Why were Americans reputed to be so highly materialistic? Society in North America was exceptionally fluid. Such a culturally diverse and geographically mobile population could not establish and maintain the traditional status symbols rooted in ancient lineages and hereditary rights in Britain. A never-ending stream of newcomers reinforced the colonials' need for inexpensive, movable, and fashionable objects. Standardized consumer goods and rules for using them gave immigrants of means confidence that their rank would be recognized immediately no matter where they traveled or settled in polite society. Those who owned the "right stuff" without knowing how to use it properly gave themselves away as imposters. The new material culture divided the haves from the have-nots and the knowledgeable from the know-nothings. Traditionalists, the poor, and most slaves usually continued to practice their customary folkways.

The eighteenth-century consumer revolution was on view everywhere in Williamsburg. Aspiring ladies and gentlemen wore London fashions purchased from Jane and Margaret Hunter's millinery shop or tailored by Severinus Durfey and laundered by Ann Ashby. They learned the rules of courtesy, the art of polite conversation, the fine points of decorating their homes, and the customs of the dinner and tea table. They participated in genteel pastimes. The fashion-conscious populace attended playhouses, concerts, and scientific lectures. They hired dancing masters, teachers, lawyers, doctors, and other providers of specialized services. Women in the middling rank and above were particularly affected by material and behavioral changes. Those who aspired to gentility, such as Annabelle Powell, assumed household duties and obligations that become much more numerous and complex as they engaged in elaborate social activities and as their standards of living improved. Educating children, especially daughters, and training household slaves in appropriate skills and deportment also demanded more of the housewife's attention.

The Art of Dressing Fish, by Johann Elias Haid after a painting by Johann Kasper Heilman, black and white mezzotint engraving, Augsburg, Germany, 1773. This housewife presents a genteel appearance even in the midst of domestic chores.

The consumer revolution rebuilt Williamsburg by replacing the earliest rustic and dilapidated structures with the "neat and plain" formal buildings that gave the town a totally different appearance after 1750. Henry Wetherburn exemplified this trend by adding a "great room" for the entertainment of large groups to his tavern at mid-century. While Williamsburg could never compete with the grandeur of cities like Philadelphia and Charleston, contemporaries regarded Virginia's capital as a fashion center. It was a favorite meeting place for William Byrd II and other members of the homegrown gentry known as "the river aristocracy." Thomas Jefferson remembered Williamsburg as "the finest school of manners and morals that ever existed in America."

Although towns and townspeople changed first and most drastically, new patterns of consumption were not confined to urban places and urban residents. While towns like Williamsburg served as the model for the fashion conscious in Virginia, some quite ordinary residents of the countryside demanded some of the same kinds of consumer goods to mark their rising economic and social positions.

SELLING RESPECTABILITY—RETAILING AND PRODUCTION

England established the colony of Virginia to exploit the region's natural resources, including its agricultural products. When John Rolfe introduced West Indian tobacco, the tremendous profits it earned on the European market altered the colony's economy forever. Tobacco sales enabled Virginians to purchase manufactured goods from England. Beginning in the 1660s, the

Navigation Acts strengthened this trade relationship by eliminating competition since Virginians could import goods only through British merchants.

The Tobacco Inspection Act of 1730 guaranteed the quality of tobacco and centralized its collection at inspection warehouses. It also encouraged the development of permanent retail businesses throughout the colony. Merchants, particularly the Scots, promptly established networks of stores where tobacco was purchased and imported goods could be sold year round to customers in the neighborhood. A small planter did not have to sell his tobacco when the annual fleet arrived. Instead, he could use tobacco notes from the warehouses to establish credit and purchase goods at any time. The notes were readily transferable so planters could bargain with several merchants at different locations. As a result, stores sprang up everywhere. By the middle of the eighteenth century, complex distribution and credit systems had developed throughout Tidewater, Southside, and Piedmont Virginia.

The network of stores that developed in colonial Virginia was a part of the expanding commercial system that made consumer goods widely available throughout England and its empire. Technological innovations spun off from the seventeenth-century scientific revolution helped to supply a worldwide market, as did more efficient organization of labor and new marketing practices. Extensive industrial changes in eighteenth-century England began in the textile industry where mechanization and waterpower increased pro-

Cartouche from *A Map of the most Inhabited part of Virginia . . .* , by Joshua Fry and Peter Jefferson, hand-colored line engraving, England, 1751. Courtesy, Swem Library, College of William and Mary, Williamsburg, Va. Slaves load tobacco for shipment to England; in return, Virginians ordered manufactured goods.

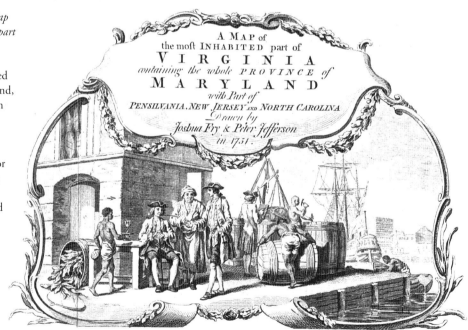

duction, especially of cotton yarns. Advances in ceramic technology led to more quickly changing designs and higher-quality wares. Innovations in mining, including the use of Newcomen's pump to drain deep mines, opened new supplies of coal, a cheap, plentiful fuel that increased productivity in industries such as iron smelting and ceramics manufacture.

While technological developments resulted in direct improvements in specific industries, most products continued to be made using traditional workbench tools and technologies. Yet many industries in England were revolutionized in other ways. Entrepreneurs reorganized small workshops so that tradesmen produced goods collaboratively. Production became more specialized, each individual artisan working on one piece or performing one operation of the complicated process. Masters coordinated production, supplied raw materials, set quotas, enforced standards, collected the finished goods, and oversaw wholesale marketing.

Whether technical or economic, innovations in production were practical only because markets had grown large enough to support them. Markets in England expanded throughout the century as the demand for attractive, inexpensive manufactured goods and newfangled foodstuffs spread throughout the kingdom and beyond. Canals and improved roads were built to carry goods to every corner of the realm. Advances of all kinds made English manufactures noteworthy for their high quality, wide variety, and good prices. Overseas markets also grew enormously. By the time of the Revolution, North America in particular had become a major consumer of English goods.

Competition was stiff. Virginia merchants ran long newspaper advertisements describing their merchandise in detail. To attract and keep their clientele, merchants redesigned their stores to display their wares more enticingly. They stocked a wide assortment of goods to appeal to all tastes and pocketbooks. Pricing became more competitive, bringing new products and new styles within the reach of many more consumers. In the absence of a banking system in the colony, Williamsburg storekeepers such as William Prentis and John Greenhow were obliged to extend credit in order to attract and keep customers.

Perhaps because the gentry regularly gathered in the capital, more tradespeople there than in other Virginia towns manufactured fashion and luxury goods. Newly arrrived artisans usually had been trained in London or in provincial British cities. Style-conscious patrons—from planter George Washington to saddler Alexander Craig—supported local cabinetmakers, upholsterers, carvers, carpenters, masons, jewelers, watch- and clockmakers, engravers, milliners, glovers, hatters, mantua makers, staymakers, and other manufacturers of stylish goods.

Local shops and warerooms displayed up-to-date fashions, and the tradesmen themselves were purveyors of new styles. Dressing and behaving much like their clientele, smart business people educated their customers in new

Elijah Boardman, by Ralph Earl, oil on canvas, America, 1789. Courtesy, Metropolitan Museum of Art, New York, N. Y., bequest of Susan W. Tyler. For business reasons, this merchant in his counting room and other tradesmen kept up with the latest fashions and etiquette.

trends. Nevertheless, retailers' influence in matters of taste was tempered by what their customers would accept.

To enlarge their product line and increase the number of potential customers, some entrepreneurial craftsmen engaged in several related trades at the same time. Benjamin Bucktrout, for example, made furniture, repaired spinets and harpsichords, and hung wallpaper. Another cabinetmaker silvered glass for mirrors in addition to performing more typical furniture construction work. To keep up with new skills and to offer more variety, tradesmen sometimes associated themselves with those in related crafts. Coachmakers employed gilders, wheelwrights, and blacksmiths. Carvers worked with cabinetmakers, and engravers worked with silversmiths. Such collaborations expanded the range of styles and products that a single shop could offer.

Lawyers, doctors, music teachers, artists, and others offering services also settled in the Virginia capital. Customers paid them good money for intangibles—their advice and expertise. A novice would gladly pay a dancing master for professional instruction in the intricacies of the minuet if he or she hoped to attract the notice of polished company at balls and assemblies. Many who purchased genteel services were certainly ladies and gentlemen, while other customers such as silversmith James Geddy and cabinetmaker Anthony Hay belonged to the prosperous middling sort.

"China Tables," pl. LI in Thomas Chippendale, *The Gentleman and Cabinet-Maker's Director,* 1st ed. (London, 1754). Williamsburg cabinetmakers excelled in making elaborate tea tables.

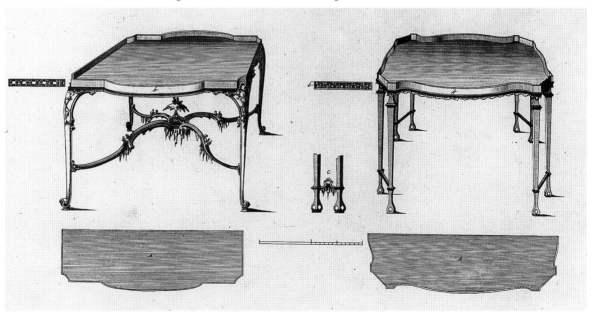

Although international standards of fashion prevailed, there was still room for a modicum of local preference and individual expression. Williamsburg was a center of fashion in Virginia, but nonetheless some provincialisms remained popular in the colonial capital. Most frame houses, for example, were painted a single color, typically white or Spanish brown. Local furniture makers generally worked in the "neat and plain" style rather than richly ornamenting their pieces, although eastern Virginia tea tables frequently display lavish carving. As a rule, however, Virginia fashions reflected current European styles.

DEMOCRATIZATION

Because new goods were available to anyone with money in his or her pocket, participation in consumer culture laid the groundwork for democracy. Respectability acquired from stores, teachers, and books strengthened one of the ideas that underpinned the Revolution: the belief in every person's equal worth and in his or her right to a better life. Recently, some historians have begun to see the consumer revolution as one of the earliest and strongest alternatives to traditional ideas about a God-given social order and about the deference that most men and all women were expected to pay to their natural superiors. The full fruits of that birthright, which still are not enjoyed by all citizens today, were certainly unimagined by most Americans in the period we interpret at Colonial Williamsburg. Notwithstanding, the idea took root in the common pleasures and everyday purchases that more and more townspeople came to enjoy after about 1730.

Owning land or personal property gave planters and tradesmen a stake in society and entitled them to vote. Widespread possession of fashionable, status-giving objects granted a nation of newcomers unusually easy access to social and political systems. Those who moved to Virginia and other colonies by choice viewed their new home as the "land of opportunity." (Africans, of course, came by force, not by choice.) America was renowned as "the best poor man's country" for its abundance of land and because the social order was not yet sharply delineated. A shortage of skilled labor in the colonies meant better wages for those with training and experience.

As stylish living spread to the "middling sort," the newly established popular press flooded the market with prints, plays, novels, broadsides, and books on self-improvement. The public's appetite for the "freshest Advices, Foreign and Domestick" created a mass market for information and a brand-new retail market all its own. Never had so many been willing to pay for useful information. Nor had so many been eager to sell it at affordable prices. In Williamsburg, the Printing Office supplied the public with polite literature and practical information by selling imported and locally produced books and printing the weekly *Virginia Gazette*. Expanding avenues of communica-

High Life Below Stairs, by John Collett, oil on canvas, London, 1763. In their own ways, servants attempted to emulate their masters' way of dressing and behaving.

tion brought about a new phenomenon—widespread discussion of numerous topics from fashion to politics. Newspapers and broadsides printed everything from the arrival of a shipment of store goods and the play premiering at the theater down the block to the latest gossip and the most recent acts of Parliament. Easy access to printed materials at low prices greatly enlarged the number of those in the know. As more people became better informed about the issues of the day, power relationships in families, communities, and politics began to change.

As the consumer impulse moved down the social ladder, nearly everyone adopted materialistic values. Modern measures of individual worth gradually replaced traditional ones. In practice, these values manifested themselves differently from place to place and among people of different ranks, thereby giving rise to adaptations and social variations. Those with leaner pocketbooks could still acquire the trappings of gentility through the purchase of second-hand goods at estate auctions or elsewhere. Still, their access to respectability depended on where they lived and how much time could be devoted to polishing their manners.

CLASHING INTERESTS

Social mobility and pleasure-seeking—and what else motivates materialists?—have seldom taken place without a clash of interests. Those who clamor to share America's bounty more widely have often been opposed by the forces of selfishness and exclusivity. One person's happiness usually has come out of someone else's pocket or someone else's hide. The "Buying Respectability" story line is full of adversaries, starting with the rich and poor.

Slave labor financed the consumer revolution in Virginia. African-Americans worked in the tobacco fields, built and tended the great houses, and practiced skilled trades. Slaves were simultaneously symbols, commodities, and the means of production in the drive for wealth and respectability. Did the spread of genteel culture set up rivalries and divisions within the slave community? Did it create a double identity for black cooks, musicians, coachmen, and body servants who served fashion-conscious masters and mistresses but who inevitably were also part of the culture of the quarter? Historians can only speculate.

Some slaves bought or borrowed fashionable items for their own use. A traveler wrote of his surprise upon seeing "in the midst of poverty some cups and a teapot" at the Mount Vernon slave quarter. Did consumer goods have the same meaning for enslaved Virginians as for free African-Americans? The few probate inventories left by free blacks show that some owned stylish goods. For example, local African-American carter Matthew Ashby owned a tea board and a silver watch.

The Old Plantation, maker unknown, watercolor on laid paper, America, 1790–1800. Slaves participated in two kinds of cultures— European fashions (clothing and jewelry) and African traditions (music and dance).

Conservative folkways still flourished in eighteenth-century Virginia, especially in the countryside. German immigrants in the valley of Virginia, for example, were slower to accept a way of life that smacked of English superiority. Some Ulster Scots, Baptists, Quakers, poor farmers, certain free blacks, and other plain people were indifferent to or outright scornful of newfangled upstarts whom they increasingly identified as town dwellers or planters too big for their britches.

Traditionalists were not alone in their concern that keeping up with the Joneses would subvert both the moral and the social order. Preachers, playwrights, and politicians decried the "frenzy of fashion." Debates about the insidious spread of luxury appeared in the pages of the *Virginia Gazette.* The topic was disputed in Williamsburg taverns. Clergy condemned excessive luxury from the pulpit at Bruton Parish Church, while Baptist preachers warned their congregations about self-indulgence and castigated the gentry for their spendthrift ways. The growing demand for consumer goods intensified competition among storekeepers. It raised the stakes in the old game of one-upmanship. Rather than meekly accepting their husbands' choices, wives increasingly insisted on having a say in decisions about the purchase of household goods and clothing.

American prosperity prompted a series of political crises between England and her colonies. In the decade leading up to the Revolution, Parliament looked to the New World to help pay imperial debts and passed the Townshend Duties and the Tea Act taxing a variety of imported commodities. Colonists relied on British imports but took offense at such taxation.

Detail from *The Sleeping Congregation,* by William Hogarth, print, England, 1736. Some clergymen frowned on their flocks' materialism.

Trade goods became the focus of political discontent, thereby creating new consumer pressures in the colony. Some protested British tyranny and showed solidarity with their fellow colonists by denying themselves foreign goods and supporting a ban on imports. Others redirected their business to local tradesmen sympathetic to American interests. Speaker Randolph's household items reflected his political sympathies. He bought Irish linen, curtained his bedstead with Virginia cloth, and drank legal coffee instead of boycotted tea. Peer pressure had its effect as well. John Greenhow explained in an advertisement that the tea he sold had been imported before the Nonimportation Association. Rival storekeeper John Prentis apologized in the *Gazette* for violating the nonimportation agreement by ordering the tea that protesters dumped in the York River. Those who attended the "homespun ball" at the Capitol proudly gave up brocades and laces in the American cause.

In Virginia, formal institutions—courthouses and churches—were relatively weak, while informal ones—social occasions and public gatherings—were relatively strong in spreading respectability. Consumer goods and services left their mark on everything from private entertainments to retail stores to dances and theatrical performances. Strict protocols governed travel, public entertainments, business dealings, marriages, burials, education, the practice of religion, and much more. Each activity required the proper apparel, equipment, and social setting. Buildings with new parlors, dining rooms, or assembly rooms began to appear in colonial towns, including Williamsburg, in the mid-eighteenth century. Carefully designed social spaces separated knowledge-

"No Stamp Act" teapot, creamware, England, 1765. Tea became a rallying point in revolutionary issues. This teapot proclaims a decidedly pro-American sentiment.

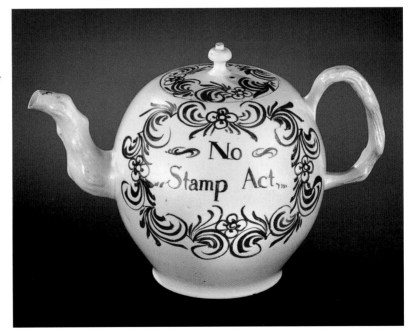

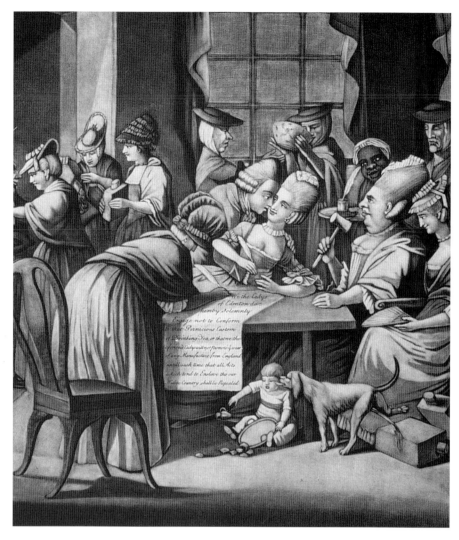

A Society of Patriotic Ladies, At Edenton in North Carolina, by P. Dawe, print, London, 1775. The ladies of Edenton, N. C., patriotically forsake drinking tea.

able and respectable citizens from their socially untutored inferiors. Thus the consumer revolution helped create the perception among traditionalists that formal institutions encouraged exclusion rather than inclusion. Private and public tensions between economic and social ranks, races, genders, New Light and Old Light Christians, and country and city became apparent everywhere.

COMING OF THE REVOLUTION

The development of the consumer society influenced the American Revolution in a number of ways. Recent research shows that the consumer revolution even gave voice to Americans' growing conflict with Britain. Many colonists came to believe that their "insatiable itch for merchandizing" and their folly and extravagance in imitating foreign fashions had set up the constitutional conflict with Parliament over issues of taxation. True or not, conspicuous consumption of British manufactured goods gave credence to stories of untold American wealth spread by travelers and army officers returning to Britain from the French and Indian War. The Stamp Act crisis and the Townshend Duties helped many Americans in all thirteen colonies recognize their common cause as consumers of British imports and as victims of British taxes. The nonimportation movements of 1765, 1768–1769, and 1774–1776 proved that customers in the colonies could exert economic pressure on Parliament to force change. Communal sacrifices during the boycotts brought together farmers and artisans, merchants and planters, northerners and southerners, and old money and new.

The widely shared democratic experience of consumption enabled these unlikely allies to express with one voice their anger at Parliament and their resolve to oppose its unjust laws. Joining together in a revolutionary cause eroded the stubborn localism of earlier times and gave rise to a heightened awareness of national identity. Patrick Henry put into words what many colonists were thinking when he declared, "I am no longer a Virginian, I am an American."

CONCLUSION

The influx of European peoples to the American colonies that helped to fuel the consumer revolution increased in both speed and volume during the nineteenth and twentieth centuries. Industrialization, abundant western lands, improved transcontinental transportation, and extreme geographical mobility opened limitless opportunities for industrious, risk-taking individuals. Inspired by a new republican optimism, Americans came to believe that everyone had an equal claim to pursue material wealth, a dream that united a nation of immigrants into a democracy of fellow consumers. The notion of a classless society assumed the dimensions of an American myth as fortune seekers were as likely to strike it rich as old wealthy families were to go bust. In reality, however, materialistic values attached to social status in the United States sharpened class differences by making them more visible and pervasive. In this country sooner than others, an upper class of purveyors and possessors learned to manipulate and control the economically disadvantaged in new and powerful ways.

"Buying Respectability" and the "Becoming Americans" Theme

Diverse Peoples

Large numbers of ordinary Americans—men and women, native-born and immigrants, free and enslaved—participated to some degree in the international consumer culture by the middle of the eighteenth century. For the first time in history, consumption of luxuries and amenities was not confined to the aristocracy. The middling sorts, especially townspeople, eagerly acquired the new goods and rules of gentility that went with them. Williamsburg was a magnet for those seeking their fortunes. The upper classes enjoyed the leisure, resources, and opportunities to achieve the genuine refinements of mind and character that had always distinguished true ladies and gentlemen. Others copied the fashions and aped the manners of their betters in their scramble to climb higher up the social ladder. Still others farther down the social scale, including some slaves, made no claim to gentility itself but found such means as they could to indulge in some of its amenities—a cup of tea, a bit of ribbon, a pair of gloves, and maybe a table fork instead of fingers. What these items meant to people of African descent and how they used them are still under investigation.

Once introduced to European manufactured goods, Native Americans demanded a steady supply and expanded their hunting grounds to provide Europeans with deer hides and beaver skins. Eventually, capitalistic market forces altered gender roles in Indian society by giving new importance to men's work and devaluing women's.

Clashing Interests

The new values communicated through store-bought goods sharpened the differences between the haves and have-nots and often came into conflict with traditional ideas and practices. Plain people either disdained or disregarded the newfangled upstarts. The unquenchable appetite for material goods, according to society's self-appointed guardians, subverted the moral and social order. Sermons, plays, and political debates debunked the new materialism. By the 1760s, the constitutional conflict with Parliament over taxation on imported goods that had long since become necessities grew into a classic conflict between tax resisters and those who argued that the high cost of defending the British Empire in America from its French and Indian enemies should be borne by those who enjoyed its protection.

SHARED VALUES

By the Revolution, most Americans aspired to a piece of this new store-bought culture and met little resistance beyond the nagging of preachers and the spoofing of playwrights. Folkways blended with genteel culture to create hybrid American forms of polite behavior. These compromises gave substance to the popular notion that every free white citizen enjoyed a rough-and-ready equality. The gathering conflict with Great Britain over the Stamp Act and the Townshend Duties helped Americans throughout the thirteen colonies recognize their shared experience as common consumers of British goods and common victims of the higher taxes Parliament attached to some of those goods. Nonimportation movements in the 1760s and '70s brought together planters, craftsmen, storekeepers, housewives, gentry, and yeomanry. This democratic experience enabled the colonists to unite in opposition to Parliament and its unjust laws. The nonimportation crisis helped consumers see themselves as a larger collective, which they called "the public."

FORMATIVE INSTITUTIONS

Political institutions in the capital city of Williamsburg and the social activities they sponsored reinforced by example the image of the town's elite. Ballrooms, assembly rooms, parlors, and dining rooms were formative institutions no less than courthouses and churches. A person's appearance and deportment during Publick Times influenced marriage prospects, political clout, and business opportunities. The town was also rich in less formal institutions including schools, playhouses, and dancing and music lessons that taught the rules of refined conduct and rehearsed their practice.

PARTIAL FREEDOMS

Knowing the rules and owning the "right stuff" required leisure, education, and resources. The wealthy enjoyed those advantages disproportionately to the poor. While the consumer revolution brought higher standards of living to many ordinary people, traditional notions of social hierarchy changed slowly. Materialistic values attached to social position in the new United States heightened class divisions by making them obvious and unavoidable.

REVOLUTIONARY PROMISE

The domination of the rich over the poor is not the end of the story. Inexpensive consumer goods, the things they could do, and the harmless human pleasures they provided became for many the fullest expression of their liberal Jeffersonian right to the pursuit of happiness. Easy access to consumer goods and cosmopolitan services has been a tremendous liberating force in American society. Plentiful and affordable creature comforts have oiled the wheels of democracy far more than political philosophies. In the process, this enduring American dream has been a potent catalyst dissolving people's traditional loyalties to clans, social rank, religions, and homelands.

CONNECTIONS TO OTHER "BECOMING AMERICANS" STORY LINES

TAKING POSSESSION

Manufactured goods followed the moving frontier in pack trains, peddlers' wagons, and later canal boats. Personal possessions and conduct announced one's social position to any community of strangers. Native Americans' reliance on trade goods also played an enormously important part in Euro-Indian relations, and they refashioned Native American material cultures in complex and unexpected ways. Native Americans were beset by market forces driven by the Europeans' need for pelts. Supplying that demand drastically altered Indian cultural traditions by devaluing women's work in comparison to men's. Here in Williamsburg, Native Americans sold their pottery to Governor Botetourt's staff at the Palace. The Brafferton at the College of William and Mary was established with the explicit intent of "civilizing" native boys.

ENSLAVING VIRGINIA

The extravagance indulged in by a few and the comfortable sufficiency enjoyed by many more white Virginians were made possible by the labor of Virginia's enslaved population. Their work enhanced masters' stylish appearances. Slave craftsmen helped build the great houses, the settings in which the gentry displayed the refinements that set them above lesser folk. Not to put too fine a point on it, chattel slaves were themselves as much consumer goods as a tea service. Complicating the story even more, slaves sometimes participated in consumer culture, either for their own benefit or at the direction of their masters. More background is needed on material culture in Africa during the seventeenth and eighteenth centuries in order to amplify our understanding of African-American material culture practices. Archaeologists have identified artifacts from slave sites in Virginia that include surprisingly stylish items such as ceramics and buttons, but their meanings to slaves remain obscure. People routinely denied the basic freedom to enjoy the rewards of their labor may have attached very different values to such objects, however acquired.

Redefining Family

Gentility refashioned family life and redefined relationships between husbands and wives. Women particularly felt the repercussions of the consumer revolution as more elaborate lifestyles multiplied their household chores and responsibilities. As children were expected to learn more, parents spent larger sums on their education as well as for instruction in dancing, music, and etiquette. New products were developed for a completely new set of customers; shrewd tradesmen created toys, books, and games for children. Rituals such as marriages, baptisms, and funerals became occasions for public display and generated their own specialized clothing, gifts, foods, and practices.

Choosing Revolution

Many of the thematic links between the "Buying Respectability" and "Choosing Revolution" story lines are described in the "Coming of the Revolution" section. But the war was not the last chapter in the larger story. Almost as soon as hostilities ceased, English merchants and manufacturers rushed to reopen the American market. The new nation inspired new product lines bearing American symbols such as George Washington and American eagles. These goods were often designed and made in England specifically for export to the United States.

Freeing Religion

The sin of pride and its affront to Christian humility were defining issues in the religious life of America. The pursuit of materialism contradicted both the traditional notion of propriety and the newly awakened dedication to austerity and self-sacrifice.

Story Line Team: Pam Pettengell, Liza Gusler, Mack Headley, Rick Hill, Mark Howell, Bill Pittman, Emma L. Powers, Susan Shaeff, and Paul Scott.

Further Reading

Borsay, Peter. *English Urban Renaissance: Culture and Society in the Provincial Town, 1660–1770.* Oxford: Clarendon Press, 1989.

Breen, T. H. "An Empire of Goods: The Anglicization of Colonial America, 1690–1776." *Journal of British Studies,* XXV (1986), pp. 467–499.

_____. "Narrative of Commercial Life: Consumption, Ideology, and Community on the Eve of the American Revolution." *William and Mary Quarterly,* 3rd Ser., L (1993), pp. 471–501.

Brewer, John, and Roy Porter, eds. *Consumption and the World of Goods.* London: Routledge, 1993.

Bushman, Richard L. *The Refinement of America. Persons, Houses, Cities.* New York: Alfred A. Knopf, 1992.

Carson, Cary, Ronald Hoffman, and Peter J. Albert, eds. *Of Consuming Interests. The Style of Life in the Eighteenth Century.* Charlottesville, Va.: University Press of Virginia, 1994.

Crowley, John E. *The Invention of Comfort: Sensibilities and Design in Early Modern Britain and Early America.* Baltimore, Md.: Johns Hopkins University Press, 2001.

Hunter, Phyllis Whitman. *Purchasing Identity in the Atlantic World: Massachusetts Merchants, 1670–1780.* Ithaca, N. Y.: Cornell University Press, 2001.

Martin, Ann Smart. "Makers, Buyers, and Users. Consumerism as a Material Culture Framework." *Winterthur Portfolio,* XXVIII (1993), pp. 141–157.

Mason, Frances Norton, ed. *John Norton & Sons, Merchants of London and Virginia; Being the Papers from the Counting House for the Years 1750 to 1795.* New York: Augustus M. Kelley, 1968.

McKendrick, Neil, John Brewer, and J. H. Plumb. *The Birth of a Consumer Society: The Commercialization of Eighteenth-Century England.* Bloomington, Ind.: Indiana University Press, 1982.

Shammas, Carole. "Explaining Past Changes in Consumption and Consumer Behavior." *Historical Methods,* XXII (1989), pp. 61–67.

_____. *The Pre-Industrial Consumer in England and America.* Oxford: Clarendon Press, 1990.

Walsh, Lorena S. "Fettered Consumers: Slaves and the Anglo-American 'Consumer Revolution.'" Paper presented at the annual meeting of the Economic History Association, 1992, copy, Foundation Library, Colonial Williamsburg Foundation.

This reenactment of the mid-1770s marriage of Hannah Powell and William Drew celebrates the formation of a new family.

REDEFINING
FAMILY

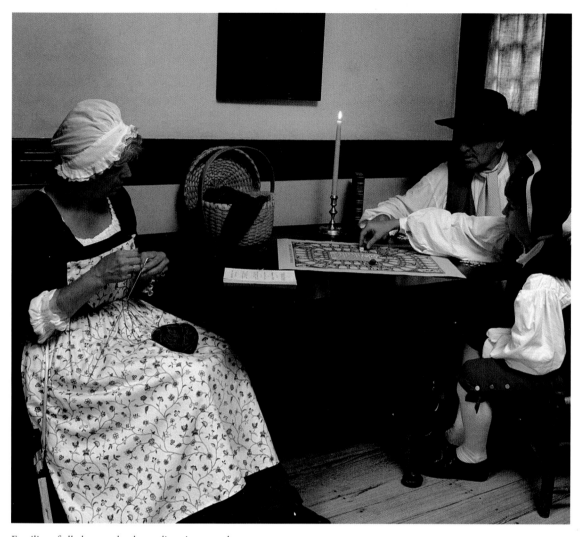

Families of all classes valued spending time together.

REDEFINING FAMILY

The "Redefining Family" story line explores the effects of changes in society between black, white, and Native American families that resulted in the development of a new American family.

KEY POINTS

- THESIS. During the eighteenth century, customs of family life inherited from Europe underwent alterations that had a profound effect on the way family members defined themselves in relation to one another and to society at large. Gradually, these changes brought the "modern American" family into being.

- THE SEVENTEENTH CENTURY. Harsh conditions of everyday life, which made the formation of stable families difficult for the first generations of European and African immigrants, began to ease by the end of the seventeenth century. Native American family patterns, by contrast, continued to be altered by disease, displacement, and warfare.

- THE WHITE FAMILY. The European family was patterned after a patriarchal ideal in which the father exercised supreme authority over an extended family, at least in theory. Reality often deviated from that ideal.

- THE NATIVE AMERICAN FAMILY. European observers misunderstood traditional Native American work and family relations, and interaction with Europeans further undermined the structure of the traditional Indian family and ultimately threatened its survival.

- THE BLACK FAMILY. Enslaved Africans, torn from their homeland and denied the stability of legal marriage, created distinctively African-Virginian family structures based on African concepts of extended kinships.

- THE FAMILY TRANSFORMED. A more openly affectionate, child-centered family that reflected egalitarian republican sentiments and changing roles for men and women began to emerge in gentry and middling white families after the middle of the eighteenth century.

- CONCLUSION. The redefined American white family became accepted as an important part of the ideal for the new American nation. Notwithstanding, some white families, especially poor whites, retained their patriarchal-based status. By contrast, Native American and African-American families remained virtually unaffected by egalitarian, republican sentiments.

BACKGROUND AND THESIS

Americans today often express concern about rapid changes overtaking the American family, changes that they believe threaten the "traditional family" and the enduring moral and cultural values it is presumed to embody. At Colonial Williamsburg, we have an opportunity to shed the light of hindsight on this discussion by helping visitors understand that the family, like other human institutions, is both an agent of change and a product of ongoing historical forces.

There has never been just one type of family. African, Native American, and European peoples have each had their own traditional family structures, ceremonies, rites of passage, and taboos. The structure of family life for all groups underwent transformations during the seventeenth and eighteenth centuries that changed the way parents and children and husbands and wives perceived themselves one to another and in relation to the larger society. Native Americans and Africans uprooted from their traditional homelands, cut off from their customary family practices, and subjected to the will of white Virginians experienced fewer opportunities to establish customary family relations and often were obliged to adapt to new circumstances or face extinction.

By the end of the eighteenth century, the white American family had begun developing a family structure that we now recognize as modern: one that was essentially nuclear, openly affectionate, child-centered, relatively egalitarian, and, at the same time, also individualistic. Such families appeared first among the gentry. Little by little, they became a model for other groups, and eventually the pattern for the modern American family, or, paradoxically, what we again often refer to as the "traditional" family.

SURVIVING THE SEVENTEENTH CENTURY

European immigration to the Chesapeake irrevocably undermined the institution of the Indian family as disease, displacement, and intensified intertribal warfare decimated native populations. Family development among transplanted African and European peoples was likewise arrested, or at least radically skewed, by the unhealthy climate and environment of the region and the demographics of the early immigration. Endemic fevers and intestinal diseases killed young and old indiscriminately. Before 1640, European immigrants to the Chesapeake, the majority of whom were male indentured servants, had a fifty-fifty chance of dying during their first year. Men outnumbered women seven to one in the early years. Long periods of indenture delayed marriage for many immigrants. A quarter of all children died before their first birthday, and half of all marriages were ended by the death of one partner before the seventh anniversary. For African immigrants, the horrors of the Middle Passage and harsh working conditions in the New World made the story even grimmer.

These circumstances populated the Virginia colony with many orphans, half-siblings, stepchildren, and foster parents. Because there were more men than women and because wives typically survived their husbands, white women enjoyed unusual opportunities to head households and accumulate property in their own names. One historian even speaks of a seventeenth-century "widow-archy."

The increasing institutionalization of slavery as defined by Virginia law shaped the development of the African family. A 1662 statute decreed that the freedom or slavery of the mother determined the status of a black child. Subsequent laws restricted interracial marriage, limited the rights of free mulatto children, and encouraged the harsh punishment of slaves. Legislation further defined the differences between black and white family life and reaffirmed the power of the white master.

Conditions that adversely affected the family formation of Virginia-born black and white settlers began to improve by the end of the seventeenth century. For instance, life expectancy rose, and the numbers of men and women grew more equal. The Virginia-born white population began to replace itself. Marriages of whites took place earlier, lasted longer, and produced larger numbers of surviving children. Increasingly stable conditions promoted a more normal course of family development.

THE FUNCTION OF THE FAMILY

Historically, the family was the basic political, religious, social, and economic unit in society, and, as such, both a public and a private institution. It educated the young, served as the first level of government, and cared for the sick, the elderly, and the disabled. Any family that we portray here in Williamsburg was involved in one or all of these essential functions. Their specific ideas about families and their customs of family life varied with each cultural group—African, European, or Native American.

THE PATRIARCHAL IDEAL

The traditional ideal of family structure that British immigrants brought to Virginia was a patriarchal hierarchy where the father figure held a position of supreme authority over his wife, children, and all other dependents living in the household. This concept of authority and dependency defined the family. Everyone subject to the authority of the householder was considered a member of the family—immediate relatives, dependent kin, hired help, tenants, indentured servants, apprentices, and slaves.

Patriarchal authority served the dynastic aspirations of some wealthy

"Colonel Charles Carter of Cleve," maker unknown, oil on canvas, Virginia, ca. 1725. Charles Carter and his wife (*right*) depict how wealthy Virginians chose to be viewed during the second quarter of the eighteenth century. As patriarch, Carter exerted control over both his land and his extended family.

"Mrs. Charles Carter of Cleve" (probably Anne Byrd Carter), by William Dering, oil on canvas, Virginia, 1735–1740. Mrs. Carter's life revolved around her family and the domestic duties that supported her husband's position.

Virginia planters by perpetuating the power and influence of the house or lineage. Most important was preserving the ownership of family lands intact. The customs of primogeniture (inheritance by the eldest son) and entail (legal proscription against the sale or grant of land outside the lineage) supported the dynastic ambitions of the gentry. The right of fathers to will land to their sons when they came of age or married reinforced the patriarch's authority. Daughters' inheritances and marriage gifts usually took the form of slaves and livestock rather than land.

These dynastic planter families developed extensive and interwoven kinship networks that protected family wealth and concentrated political power in family hands. The political structure of the colony was inextricably linked to the kinship shared by its leading families that ranged all the way from county offices to the Virginia Council. For example, the extended Blair family of Williamsburg provided leaders to the college, the Council, the church, and the local courts. Additionally, kin ties connected the Blairs to many other influential families in the immediate Williamsburg community and throughout the colony.

Small planters and many artisans and shopkeepers in Williamsburg built a sense of family through work. Home and workplace were frequently housed under the same roof or in adjacent buildings. Here the patrimony bequeathed to children was the craft or business skills that earned the family's income. For people like the Geddys, the family was a production unit in which roles were determined by age and sex and where apprentices, slaves, and journeymen were no less important to economic success than parents and children.

An individual could be a member of several families during his or her lifetime. One might grow up in one family, apprentice in another, work as a journeyman or maidservant in another, set up a business, get married and become head or mistress of one's own family, and in old age become a dependent in someone else's home. When young Daniel Hoye was apprenticed to Williamsburg artisan Benjamin Powell in the early 1750s, he left the home of the Warwick County family he had been born into, moved to Williamsburg, and became part of the Powell family. After several years of service to Mr. Powell, Hoye established himself as a wheelwright, married, and started his own family.

The social, cultural, and business opportunities available in the capital attracted large numbers of single young people to Williamsburg. Apprentices, including orphan apprentices from England such as Thomas Everard and William Prentis, young single women such as Elizabeth Wythe's niece Mary Taliaferro and Betty Randolph's niece Elizabeth Harrison, and college students such as Thomas Jefferson and Nathaniel Burwell boarded with Williamsburg families for varying lengths of time. Some of them married here and remained in the Williamsburg area.

Whether as large as a family dynasty or as modest as a tradesman's household, the patriarchal system replicated the structure and reinforced the authority of the state. A father's role and responsibilities in the family mirrored in miniature the patriarchal relationship of a monarch to his people.

THE PATRIARCHAL REALITY

While theory held that patriarchal authority resided in a male head of the family, reality did not always follow suit. The role of women often extended beyond their traditional domestic sphere, important as that was in its own right. Although society expected young white women to marry, several spinsters (including English milliners Margaret and Jane Hunter) established prosperous businesses in Williamsburg. Jane later married wigmaker Edward Charlton and launched a rival millinery shop across the street.

Ordinary tradesmen and small planters depended on the labor of their wives and children in the workshop or in the field. A serious illness or the death of a husband or father often reversed traditional roles and created situations where the "patriarch" of the family was, in fact, a woman. Clementina Rind assisted her husband, William, public printer and editor of the *Virginia Gazette*. Later, she assumed these duties single-handedly during his illness and took over the printing business after William's death. At the same time, Clementina also reared their five children until she died the following year.

While coping with the emotional stress occasioned by the loss of a husband, widows often had to deal with financial crises caused by the loss of family income. On learning that her husband's estate was deeply in debt, Elizabeth Hay, widow of Raleigh Tavern owner and keeper Anthony Hay, renounced her legacy and claimed her widow's dower (the common rights of a widow to a life interest of one-third of her husband's pre-debt property). That recourse brought greater advantages to Elizabeth and her children. Likewise, Anne Geddy became the guardian of her children and was solely responsible for their welfare and education. As femme sole executrix of her husband's estate, she was able to bring legal action and conduct business in her own right.

Young widows in colonial Virginia typically remarried quickly; older widows often remained single and exercised the power due to heads of households. Living in Williamsburg made it easier for a widow to avoid remarriage because nearby friends provided support and the bustling life of the town afforded economic opportunities. Widows such as midwife Catherine Blaikley and tavern keepers Jane Vobe and Christiana Campbell became successful businesswomen. Widow Ann Wager decided to leave her position as private

"Relieur," in Denis Diderot and Jean d'Alembert, eds., *Encyclopédie, ou Dictionnaire Raisonné des Sciences, des Arts et des Métiers, par un Société de Gens de Lettres* (Paris, 1751–1765), Vol. VIII, pl. I. Towns like Williamsburg provided opportunities for employment to women who either supported themselves or supplemented the income of their husbands.

tutor at Carter's Grove plantation and take employment as mistress of the Bray School in Williamsburg.

Women often turned to networks of family and friends during times of illness and family need. Teenager Frances Baylor Hill of Hillsborough plantation stayed with her sister during the days before her sister's death following childbirth and then was one of the family members who stood for the christening of the baby. Living in Williamsburg made such arrangements more convenient.

Although not all marriages were happy, divorce was not an alternative in colonial Virginia. Couples with marital problems had only a few choices— apply to the court for a separation (seldom requested), work them out, put up with them, or separate without a legal agreement.

The death of one or both parents happened frequently in the Chesapeake colonies. Virginia passed legislation that provided for the care and education of orphans as early as the 1640s. Orphans with assets received an education according to the level of income that their estates could sustain. When an orphan inherited no estate or one so small it could not subsidize "book education," churchwardens bound the child out to learn a trade. Guardians were held accountable for the integrity of the orphan's estate. The law and the church supported and protected marriage and family unity for the white population.

FIRST FAMILIES OF VIRGINIA

Native American family life was both different from and transformed by contact with European culture. British observers (mostly male) regarded gender roles and marital customs among the local Powhatan Indians as an abdication of men's proper paternal authority, and they viewed the lavishly affectionate and seemingly permissive treatment of Indian children as an invitation to anarchy. Cultural blindness often misconstrued similarities in the customs of the two peoples. Whites, for example, took the Indians' courtship practice of presenting a prospective bride's family with skins or other goods as evidence that brides were bought like commodities even though it was commonplace for European and African suitors to be required to demonstrate they could support a family.

Most of the Indian cultures were matrilineal, meaning that family membership and descent were traced through the mother's side. Often a son had an especially strong relationship with a maternal uncle who took responsibility for much of his education. Married men had obligations to two households, to their wives and children on one hand and to their mothers' people on the other. Occasionally, Native American women inherited positions as rulers. Though most men had only one wife, divorce seems to have been relatively easy and considerable sexual freedom was not inconsistent with the idea of marriage. Adultery resulted only when the spouse did not sanction the liaison. Relatives showed Powhatan children much affection. Punishing children by beating them was not part of Indian culture before contact with Europeans.

Work was rigidly allocated by gender. Women bore responsibility for growing crops (though men helped clear the land), erecting houses, making household utensils, carrying burdens when the family moved, gathering firewood, and, of course, rearing children. Hunting, fishing, and waging war were the men's jobs that often took them away from home for long periods. Men also made and maintained most of the implements related to these activities.

Europeans viewed this division of labor in the light of their own preconceptions. They regarded Powhatan men as lazy and idle, engaged only in fishing or hunting, which they considered to be leisure activities, while the women were exploited and condemned to a life of drudgery. In fact, the economic contributions of both sexes were roughly equal, and Native Americans may not have viewed women's work as demeaning or less important than that of the men until later.

Cultural misunderstandings between Indians and whites were seldom bridged by well-meant attempts at indoctrination like those offered by instructors at the Indian School at the College of William and Mary. Indians showed little interest in attending the school; those who did soon returned to their native ways. Occasionally, successful students such as John Nettles and John Montour used their English education to aid their own people by becoming skilled interpreters. Generally speaking, Native Americans appear to have had little desire to acquire European culture, however much they valued some products of the white man's technology.

There were some mixed families of course. Frontiersmen sometimes married Indian women. Indians occasionally intermarried with blacks. But, despite some coincidental similarities, there is little evidence that Native American attitudes and practices were consciously included in European or African family customs.

The negative impact of the Europeans on Native American families was enormous. Disease and displacement led to high mortality and low birthrates. The establishment of white settlements disrupted the delicate system of land use on which the Indians depended. An influx of European trade goods displaced native craft technologies. The appetite of European markets for hunters' furs and hides exaggerated the importance of the male role in Indian society and devalued that of the female. Native Americans responded to these disruptive influences in many different ways, from acceptance to adaptation to resistance and outright rejection. Ultimately, unremitting pressure from European newcomers meant that the less numerous and technologically disadvantaged Indians were pushed to the brink of extinction.

Yet they managed to survive, even though their indigenous cultural patterns were distorted or destroyed. In an effort to minimize European influences, the Pamunkey Indians prohibited women married to white men from living on tribal lands as long as their marriage lasted. Nonetheless, notions of patrilineal descent and other foreign customs crept in. A visitor to the Pamunkeys in 1759 found them living in traditional Yi Hakans (temporary houses made from bent saplings covered with bark or reed mats) but wearing English clothes. Thomas Jefferson wrote in his *Notes on Virginia* that "there remain of the Mattaponies three or four men only. . . . They have lost their language and have reduced themselves to about fifty acres of Land. . . . The Pamunkies are reduced to about 10 or 12 men. . . . The older ones among them preserved their language in a small degree, which are the last vestiges on earth as far as we know, of the Powhatan language."

How Indian Mothers Carry Their Children, by Simon E. Gribelin, engraving, London, 1705, from Robert Beverley, *The History and Present State of Virginia,* ed. Louis B. Wright. Courtesy, University of North Carolina Press, Chapel Hill, N. C. Contact with whites changed Native American family life forever. The figure on the left shows clothing in transition, becoming more Western in style. The other figures depict traditional Indian style.

Traites Des Negres, engraved by Rollet after a painting by George Morland, black and white etching, Paris, 1790–1791. This depiction from an Abolitionist point of view illustrates how wrenching the separation from family members and family traditions was for captive Africans. In America, new family patterns developed that combined old ideas with new ways of dealing with the Africans' redefined world.

BLACK FAMILIES

The history of the African-Virginian family is the story of the struggle to rebuild stable family institutions to fill the emotional, cultural, and spiritual void created when African peoples were torn from their homelands. The hybrid family structures that resulted incorporated African, European, and distinctively African-Virginian elements.

Among the West African peoples from whom Virginia's slave population predominately derived, the ties of kinship operated at every level of society and in almost every aspect of an individual's life. Each person identified him- or herself as a member of a people, a clan, a family, and a household. A *people,* the national grouping, was unified by language and culture. The *clan* was the largest subdivision of a people, by definition a kinship grouping since every member of a clan traced descent from a common ancestor, either through the father's or the mother's line. The *family* included not just parents and children but also grandparents, aunts and uncles, cousins, and other relatives. The *household* was the smallest family. It was restricted to parents, children, and sometimes grandparents—what John S. Mbiti has referred to as the "family at night."

In West African families, there was a tradition of wives being subordinate to their husbands. But authority was more dispersed than it was in patriarchal European families. Parental responsibilities such as the care and education of children were shared with a broader kin group. Grandparents and other older relatives passed on family and clan history and traditional lore. A modern West African saying, "It takes a village to raise a child," sums up this intertwining of family responsibilities.

West African kinship connections extended laterally in one dimension, binding an individual to nearly everyone in the locality, and vertically (or historically), connecting the living with departed ancestors and children yet unborn. Social behavior and familial obligations were determined by the nature of kinship links between individuals since a person could have hundreds of "fathers," "mothers," "uncles," and "brothers." As a community was regarded as an organic whole bound by intricate ties among relatives, so an individual's life within that community derived its deepest meaning from its unity with the communal existence. Physical, emotional, and spiritual growth were marked by rites of passage that signified a person's progressive integration into the corporate body of kin, both living and dead.

For Africans enslaved and transported to Virginia, this web of kinship ties that gave them order, meaning, and continuity was swept away. Slaves suffered a "social death," to use historian Orlando Patterson's phrase. The challenge facing transportees was how to build kinship anew in an alien land. How much these new networks were of African origin, how much patterned on European models, how much improvised from scratch to fit the exigencies of the new land and the constraints of slavery are questions much debated by historians. They probably will continue to be.

Some, like E. Franklin Frazier, believed there was little evidence that African culture exerted any influence on the African-American family. "Probably never before in history," he wrote, "has a people been so completely stripped of its social heritage as the Negroes who were brought to America." Herbert Gutman made a more plausible argument when he proposed a four-stage process of destruction and rebirth: the initial West-African kinship patterns; their eradication by slavery and replacement by non-kin relationships with symbolic (or fictive) functions; the emergence of a truly African-American slave family and fictive kin networks; and, finally, an extension of ideas about family into a broader concept of allegiance to the black community as a whole. Whether derived from African tradition or developed from the Virginia experience, the extended kin network and the fictive kinship concept were vitally important to the African-Americans.

Efforts by seventeenth-century African immigrants to form families were hindered initially by the same high rates of mortality and skewed sex ratios that Europeans experienced. Transported African women had an unusually low birthrate, possibly due to the trauma of the Middle Passage and the harsh working conditions in Virginia, to traditionally longer nursing periods among Africans that were accompanied by sexual abstinence, or to the unwillingness of some women to bear children in servitude. The native-born population eventually began to replace itself. By the second quarter of the eighteenth century, slaves were living longer and in greater numbers. Concentrations of blacks on some of the larger plantations gave them the opportunity to develop a more stable family life and a degree of autonomy in their quarters.

For any slave, stability was temporal. The legal and religious institutions that promoted marriage and families for the dominant white population were indifferent or hostile to the preservation of the black family. Although masters sometimes encouraged slave marriages for their own convenience, such unions were not officially recognized by law or the established church. Some owners attempted to keep slave families together, but circumstances—bankruptcy or the master's death—could break them up at any time. Childless widow Betty Randolph's will mandated the dispersal of a large number of her slaves. In the second half of the century, slave couples were frequently separated from one another or from their children when white families relocated to the Piedmont or into growing towns like Richmond, Norfolk, Petersburg, Fredericksburg, Alexandria, and, until 1780, Williamsburg. Sometimes masters sold surplus slaves or hired them to owners who did not live in the immediate vicinity.

When elders transmitted orally their African heritage to youngsters, they were preparing the next generation for a lifetime of enslavement. Coping skills were passed along too.

Alexander Spotswood Payne and his Brother John Robert Dandridge Payne with their Nurse, attributed to the Payne Limner, oil on canvas, Goochland County, Va., 1790–1800. Courtesy, Virginia Museum of Fine Arts, Richmond, Va. The interaction between and mutual influence of blacks and whites began in childhood and continued throughout life.

Despite all these obstacles and uncertainties, black men and women continued to be united by marriage ceremonies that often combined African and European traditions. Husbands and wives who were owned by different masters often lived apart. Sometimes they traveled long distances at night to visit one another. This "night-walking," an institution born of necessity, used a network of foot trails that became physical evidence of the family ties that bound the black community together. The *Virginia Gazette* printed many advertisements by masters expressing their suspicions that slaves they owned had run away to join their families. These ads testify to the fact that whites recognized the reality, if not the legality, of slave family relationships and tried to cope with runaways who were determined to preserve these connections at great personal risk.

Slaves depended on their masters for food, shelter, and health care. Enforced subservience to whites led to complex relationships of authority, obligation, and family loyalty that must have required a good bit of diplomacy, resourcefulness, and skill to negotiate safely. Rural and urban slaves who served as domestics lived in close proximity to their owners, often sleeping in the house or in nearby outbuildings. Although favored house slaves often received cast-off clothing and other gifts from their owners, they were less likely to be given the traditional Sunday off enjoyed by field hands. Always at the beck and call of their masters, they had to bargain for free time to spend with their families or to visit with friends. Town slaves had greater opportunities to choose mates and to perform services that could bring them tips.

The close proximity of their living spaces increased the influence of white and black families on one another. Children of both races played together until their serious education for adult roles began around age ten. Slave girls in their early teens provided much of the child care in white gentry families. Slaves and whites continued to influence one another's work rhythms, living spaces, child-rearing practices, speech patterns, and religious sensibilities throughout their lives.

Sometimes the interconnection between a black and white family was not only a matter of dependency but also of blood. Documentation based on a variety of sources reveals that the number of mulattoes was growing in the eighteenth century. Although laws forbade marriage between blacks and whites, interracial unions had always existed. Some voluntary relationships were based on genuine affection and were of long duration. Just as often, however, the absolute authority of masters and the powerlessness of slaves led to incidents of rape and other forms of sexual exploitation. Black women had no protection or legal recourse from these indignities. Occasionally, a mulatto child, especially if the mother and father were bound by an affectionate and long-term alliance, attained tacit acceptance or a position of favor in the white master's family. John Custis's mulatto son Jack or members of the Hemings family at Monticello come to mind.

Not all African-Virginian families were enslaved in the eighteenth century. While only a handful of free blacks lived in Williamsburg, greater numbers of free blacks resided in adjoining James City and York Counties. Though they amounted to only 3 to 4 percent of the total population in eastern Virginia, some families included both slaves and free blacks.

The laws did not apply equally to free blacks and whites. Free black women over sixteen years old were tithable until 1769, a burden from which whites were exempt because white women were not tithable.

Williamsburg carter Matthew Ashby was the son of a white woman and a black man, a union that ultimately made him a free man. Since Matthew's mother was an indentured servant at the time of his birth, she was required to serve an additional five years. Matthew was indentured until he was thirty-one, not twenty-one, because his father was black. Matthew's wife, Ann, was a slave, so his children were slaves too. In 1769, Matthew purchased his wife and children from their owner; shortly thereafter, he petitioned the governor and Virginia Council for permission to manumit his family. The authorities acted favorably on Ashby's petition not long before his death in 1771.

The establishment of stable, emotionally and spiritually nurturing black families is a story of unremitting struggle against great odds. Slaves showed a tenacious determination to make something good out of the most unpromising circumstances. The successful formation of the African-American family takes its rightful place in American history beside the other stories of heroism in the "struggle to be free and equal."

THE FAMILY TRANSFORMED

During the course of the eighteenth century, relationships within gentry families underwent a fundamental change that set new standards that were gradually emulated throughout society. Historians sometimes call this phenomenon "the rise of the affectionate family." New ideals made hard work a virtue and upward mobility its just reward. Further, the nuclear family became the incubator of the republican ethos. Visitors to Colonial Williamsburg will see in the late eighteenth-century family portrayed here an early reflection of the individualistic, child-centered world of today.

THE NURTURING FAMILY

In the second half of the eighteenth century, marriages in gentry families were made for love more often than the unions between power families had been previously. A growing body of literature concerned with the quest for the one perfect partner reflected the growing importance of romance. Relations between family members became less formal and hierarchical and more openly emotional. The family turned inward, ceasing to be merely a microcosm of the larger society, and its public functions were gradually subordinated to its private ones. The family was increasingly regarded as a refuge from the strife and competition of the outside world, a haven for nobler principles of love, self-sacrifice, and devotion to spouses and children.

The traditional authoritarian role parents played gave way to affectionate bonds, while the relationship between husbands and wives became more

Children like tender Oziers, by John Faber, after a painting by Pierre Mercier, black and white mezzotint engraving, England, 1765. Women were expected to exemplify and direct the spiritual life of the household.

Rachel Weeping, by Charles Willson Peale, oil on canvas, America, 1772, enlarged, 1776. Courtesy, Philadelphia Museum of Art, Philadelphia, Pa., given by the Barra Foundation, Inc. Mourning the death of loved ones is universal. More open expressions of grief became commonplace toward the end of the eighteenth century.

companionable. Edmund Randolph acknowledged the influence his wife had over his beliefs and attitudes. St. George Tucker wrote unabashedly emotional poetry to his wife, Frances, during their courtship and marriage and memorialized her with tender sentiments after she died.

Fathers took a more active role in day-to-day child-rearing. St. George Tucker provides an excellent example. As a widower, his rules for governing the household showed Tucker's reliance on humor instead of physical punishment to mold the behavior of his children. He often referred to them playfully as "vagabonds," "rogues," "sweet brats," and even "my little monkies."

Women became more active in the spiritual direction they gave their children and servants. Obituaries of women, especially young women like Elizabeth Prentis and Frances Horrocks, emphasized the importance of faith and the value of women within a family. Death notices also reflected a more open, unrestrained grieving process.

Gifts like this "Welcome Little Stranger" pincushion commemorated and celebrated life events such as marriages and births.

CHILDHOOD ASSUMES NEW IMPORTANCE

Along with the new emphasis on emotional values came a basic change in the way children were perceived. Infants and young children became a focus of family life and their development a source of delight to adults. Parents began to give children pet names, distinctive clothing, juvenile books, playthings, and self-consciously educational experiences. A flood of books on child care and children's behavior tapped a growing interest in the art and science of child-rearing. Parents continued to believe in the importance of raising children to be upright, moral, independent members of society, so only the way in which they were educated changed.

In the middle of the eighteenth century, families typically included six to eight children despite the fact that stillbirths and miscarriages were common for both black and white women. Fear for the health of both the newborn child and its mother was part of every childbirth experience. Lying-in was a time when female relatives and friends rallied to support this important event.

Throughout history, parents have mourned the loss of a child. It was no different in the eighteenth century. The forms grieving took became more openly emotional because the importance of the individual was broadened to include children. Landon Carter noted that his slave Winny was "greatly affected" by the loss of one of her children, as was Carter himself when, a few days later, his daughter fell ill and died while he was away. The deaths of no fewer than four of Frances and Robert Carter's children must have brought great sadness to these residents of Palace Street in Williamsburg and may have been a factor in the family's decision to move back to Nomini Hall plantation.

Little Girls Playing, by D. N. Chodowiecke, engraving, in Johann Bernard Basesdow, *Elementarwerke für die Jugend*. Courtesy, National Art Gallery, London. Games, toys, and books created especially for children entertained and encouraged appropriate morals and behaviors. These little girls imitate their mothers' roles as wives, mothers, and hostesses.

THE NEW AMERICAN FAMILY

The design of houses reflected changing social relationships in the family: passages allowed for more privacy, beds were relegated to upstairs or back rooms, and entertainment spaces brought people together for dining and dancing. The socially driven demand for new domestic activities such as tea drinking led to the acquisition of the necessary "tools" to carry on those activities. Consumer goods such as tea equipages changed how family members—parents, children, slaves—used the home. Household servants enabled whites to devote more time to social activities.

A surplus of white men residing in the capital city may explain why some young women were successful in finding partners among higher social ranks. Successful artisan families in Williamsburg like the Powells and Geddys were able to marry their socially accomplished daughters into the lower gentry. Living in Williamsburg had other benefits. Parents who could afford to school their children in music, dance, and deportment had ready access to instructors and tutors in the social arts. While living in town, the Robert Carter family took advantage of these opportunities to enrich their children's education. After they returned to Nomini Hall, it was necessary to employ a live-in tutor and engage the services of an itinerant music and dance master.

The Williamsburg community illustrates a mix of status groups through marriages. Members of the prominent Blair family married both across and down the social scale. Blair women were linked to planters (George Braxton, Wilson Miles Cary, and John Banister), merchants (Armistead Burwell), and professionals (Dr. George Gilmer). Town clerk Joseph Davenport's daughters married cabinetmaker/tavern keeper Anthony Hay, merchants John Greenhow and William Holt, and printers Alexander Purdie and Augustine Davis.

The more openly affectionate, child-centered family that gained acceptance by the end of the eighteenth century struck a sympathetic chord with the nation's republican sentiments. The lessening of paternal authority paralleled the rejection of the patriarchal authority of the English monarch. The substitution of a more egalitarian ideal in place of a hierarchial one was mirrored in the more equal sharing of authority in the family. Successful middle-class families became more self-assured, less accepting of subordination, and more confident of their own values.

WAR AND THE NEW NATION FORCE FURTHER CHANGE

Family life was altered in other ways as husbands left for war while their wives at home found themselves temporarily—or sometimes permanently—single parents. St. George Tucker's letters record the strain imposed by separation. Wives' roles expanded as they assumed duties usually performed by their absent husbands. Children had to adapt to changing family conditions too. The postwar ideology of republicanism changed people's thinking about education. Mothers were expected to take primary responsibility for instructing children in the virtues necessary to a new republic; as a consequence, girls received more education.

Some families in the new nation lost rather than gained opportunities. Deprived of land, their population reduced, and important aspects of their traditional culture under assault, Native Americans were repeatedly uprooted and often obliged to create a different family life. Slave families still lacked legal rights. Eve and her son George ran away from Betty Randolph on hearing about Dunmore's Proclamation but found small comfort for their act of courage and desperation. This slave family was later split when Betty Randolph changed her will and ordered that Eve be sold rather than given to a niece along with George. The opening of the frontier and the cotton lands farther south after the Revolution meant that separation of African-American families was both distant and final.

Moving Toward Today's Family—An Epilogue

Historian Stephanie Grauman Wolf writes, "More modest nuclear families, ones that gave each of the children a chance through education, love, and a comfortable existence . . . were, in a way, the right kind of family structure for the new nation with its emphasis on individual attainment." Wolf refers to an archetype that was beginning to emerge among some white middling and gentry families toward the end of the period we interpret at Colonial Williamsburg. Over the next two hundred years, momentous changes in American society that profoundly affected families of all economic and ethnic groups continued to take place. Westward expansion, new waves of immigration, the growth (and reduction) of economic opportunity, eight wars, the abolition of slavery, the Victorian codification of behavior, the industrialization and urbanization of America, the civil rights struggle, the women's movement, the nonconformism of the tumultuous 1960s, and changes occurring in society today have all helped shape families as we now know them and the idea of family as we think it should be. Yet, behind all the apparent differences, some characteristic and important features of the modern American family are a legacy of the eighteenth century.

Untitled, by Thomas Bewick and his school, woodcut, London, ca. 1800, in *1800 Woodcuts by Thomas Bewick and His School*. The playful affection depicted in this woodcut is much like scenes in modern-day family snapshots.

"REDEFINING FAMILY" AND THE "BECOMING AMERICANS" THEME

DIVERSE PEOPLES

Native Americans, Africans, and British colonists held different cultural perceptions of the family. These understandings underwent profound alterations in response to the New World environment and in reaction to the other groups. The highly abnormal demographic conditions of the seventeenth century delayed and stunted the formation of family life, which was further reshaped when whites imported Africans to labor on their plantations. Encroaching settlement by Europeans and their slaves pushed the Indians from their traditional homelands.

CLASHING INTERESTS

Most Europeans considered Native American family customs to be outlandish and debased. As patriarchal slave masters, whites intervened profoundly and often peremptorily in the family experience of their bondsmen and imposed laws that relegated African-Virginians to the status of inferiors.

Some members of the gentry resisted the changes that affected many families by the third quarter of the eighteenth century. The friction between Landon Carter and his son and daughter-in-law may be interpreted either as a generational disagreement over family relations or as an expression of individual preferences. At all times, variations in individuals' beliefs about what a family should be added diversity to early Virginia society.

SHARED VALUES

Africans, Native Americans, and Europeans all placed a high value on children, family relationships, and kinship networks. As African-Virginians helped raise white children, lived and worked in close proximity to whites, and interacted with the master's family, accommodation between the races and an unconscious exchange of values took place. Living in Williamsburg could be a positive experience for both Sarah Trebell and her family's slave, Eady. Black and white Williamsburg children had some opportunity for schooling. After the Revolution, the adoption of a more egalitarian sharing of authority began to set a standard that was understood by all levels of society and is still perceived as important today.

Shared work in early Virginia households brought generations and races together.

Formative Institutions

While white masters began to accept the importance of slave families, neither the law nor the church sanctioned slave marriages. Legislation enforced the moral teachings of the Anglican church regarding acceptable social behavior and the treatment of dependents such as apprentices, servants, and slaves. Education was regarded as the chief means to pass one society's values and rules on to the next generation. The home was the unchallenged center for education, religious learning, and spiritual development.

Partial Freedoms

The gentry enjoyed more freedom in their family relationships by 1770, but these changing attitudes had no effect on slave families. Nor were they experienced in all white families, or even in all upper-class families. For example, although both husband and wife recognized the woman's role in a family, their lives continued to be narrowly defined and they were seldom educated to reach their full potential. The black family experience continued to lack stability. The opportunity for most black children in Williamsburg to receive some formal education faded when the Bray School closed its doors at the death of Ann Wager. Atypical masters such as George Wythe occasionally taught individual slaves to read. Few slave families responding to Dunmore's Proclamation gained their freedom. Native American families continued to be confined to reservations in the East or were pushed to the limits of the frontier in the West.

Revolutionary Promise

Even before the Revolution, changes in white family values and experiences heralded transformations. Those families with skills, material goods, and knowledge of the appropriate behaviors increased their opportunities for social mobility. Racism and lack of opportunity meant that Native American and slave families' full participation in the new republic remained an unfulfilled promise. A few slaves such as "Saul, the property of George Kelly, Esquire," whose petition was brought before the 1792 Virginia Assembly, were granted freedom for service to the revolutionary cause. Virginia law recognized that some marriages were not successful, so limited divorce became available here and also in the rest of the nation. After the war, educating children to participate in the new republic contributed to the optimistic expectations for the United States. The transformed white American family became a cornerstone of the American character.

CONNECTIONS TO OTHER
"BECOMING AMERICANS" STORY LINES

TAKING POSSESSION

Settling the land displaced Native American families and changed their economic and family patterns. Since land and labor were factors determining the success of whites, land possession was an important aspect of their family life. Settlement of the frontier altered family living patterns. For example, younger sons could own land earlier in their lives. Movement to the frontier changed family life for slaves who were forced to leave family members behind when their masters relocated. Because western settlers owned fewer slaves, family formation was difficult for those African-Virginians.

ENSLAVING VIRGINIA

Although Africans came to Virginia with concepts of family, slavery altered traditional patterns by not allowing legal marriage and separating families by gift or sale. Authority in the slave family ultimately rested with the white master, which redefined customary relationships. The close proximity of domestic blacks to white masters and mistresses in a family required accommodation on the part of both.

BUYING RESPECTABILITY

As families acquired more goods, more domestic labor, and more opportunities for lessons in deportment, music, and other genteel behaviors, interactions within the family changed. Lessons, particularly in urban Williamsburg, were available to many. The market economy recognized the importance of childhood, creating books about child care and a variety of toys, games, and publications for children. Families accumulated more goods that had to be cared for by both mistress and domestic slaves. Mistresses spent more time supervising the household, and, freed from the burden of physical labor, had more time to educate their children. These changes improved family comfort and allowed for social mobility. Consumer goods became symbols of their owners' rank in society, while the outward behaviors associated with using them indicated status.

CHOOSING REVOLUTION

The family was both the agent for and a product of the historical process. A lessening of paternalism in society at large paralleled changes in family relationships. The Revolutionary War gave wives new responsibilities in the absence of their husbands. War required children to adapt and adjust. When peace came, the new republic idealized aspects of family. Educational opportunities for females increased.

FREEING RELIGION

White women were appreciated as models for piety, guardians of family religious faith, and teachers of young Virginians. The church was responsible for the care of the dependent—the orphans and the destitute. Yet both church and law supported only white families, white apprentices, and white widows.

Story Line Team: Anne Schone, Antoinette Brennan, Pat Gibbs, George Hassell, Kimberly Ivey, Rose McAphee, Noel Poirier, Bunny Rich, Diane Schwarz, Laura Treese, Margie Weiler.

FURTHER READING

Brown, Kathleen M. *Good Wives, Nasty Wenches, and Anxious Patriarchs: Gender, Race, and Power in Colonial Virginia.* Chapel Hill, N. C.: University of North Carolina Press, 1996.

Calvert, Karin. *Children in the House: The Material Culture of Early Childhood, 1600–1900.* Boston: Northeastern University Press, 1992.

Carr, Lois Green, and Lorena S. Walsh. "Changing Lifestyles and Consumer Behavior in the Colonial Chesapeake." In *Of Consuming Interests: The Style of Life in the Eighteenth Century.* Edited by Cary Cason, Ronald Hoffman, and Peter J. Albert. Charlottesville, Va.: University Press of Virginia, 1994.

Chappell, Edward A. "Housing a Nation: The Transformation of Living Standards in Early America." In *Of Consuming Interests: The Style of Life in the Eighteenth Century.* Edited by Cary Carson, Ronald Hoffman, and Peter J. Albert. Charlottesville, Va.: University Press of Virginia, 1994.

Demos, John. *Past, Present, and Personal: The Family and the Life Course in American History.* New York: Oxford University Press, 1986.

Fithian, Philip V. *Journal and Letters of Philip Vickers Fithian: A Plantation Tutor of the Old Dominion, 1773–1774.* Edited by Hunter Dickinson Farish. Williamsburg, Va.: Colonial Williamsburg Foundation, 1957.

Garrett, Elisabeth Donaghy. *At Home: The American Family, 1750–1870.* New York: Harry N. Abrams, 1990.

Greven, Philip. *The Protestant Temperament: Patterns of Child-Rearing, Religious Experience, and the Self in Early America.* New York: Alfred A. Knopf, 1977.

Gunderson, Joan R. *To Be Useful to the World: Women in Revolutionary America, 1740–1790.* New York: Twayne Publishers, 1996.

Gutman, Herbert G. *The Black Family in Slavery and Freedom, 1750–1925.* New York: Pantheon Books, 1976.

Kulikoff, Allan. "The Origins of Domestic Patriarchy among White Families" and "Beginnings of the Afro-American Family." In *Tobacco and Slaves: The Development of Southern Cultures in the Chesapeake, 1680-1800.* Chapel Hill, N. C.: University of North Carolina Press, 1986.

Lewis, Jan. *The Pursuit of Happiness: Family and Values in Jefferson's Virginia.* Cambridge: Cambridge University Press, 1982.

Mintz, Steven, and Susan Kellogg. *Domestic Revolutions: A Social History of American Family Life.* Introduction and pp. 36–41. New York: Free Press, 1988.

Norton, Mary Beth. *Founding Mothers and Fathers: Gendered Power and the Forming of American Society.* New York: Alfred A. Knopf, 1996.

Pollock, Linda. *A Lasting Relationship: Parents and Children over Three Centuries.* Hanover, N. H.: University Press of New England, 1987.

Rountree, Helen. "Sex Roles and Family Life." Chap. 5 in *Powhatan Indians of Virginia: Their Traditional Culture.* Norman, Okla.: University of Oklahoma Press, 1989.

Shammas, Carole. "Anglo-American Household Government in Comparative Perspective." *William and Mary Quarterly,* 3rd Ser., LII (1995), pp. 104–144.

Smith, Daniel Blake. *Inside the Great House: Planter Family Life in Eighteenth-Century Chesapeake Society.* Ithaca, N. Y.: Cornell University Press, 1980.

Sobel, Mechal. *The World They Made Together: Black and White Values in Eighteenth-Century Virginia.* Princeton, N. J.: Princeton University Press, 1987.

Stanton, Luicia. *Free Some Day: The African-American Families of Monticello.* [Charlottesville, Va.]: Thomas Jefferson Foundation, 2000.

Stevenson, Brenda E. *Life in Black and White: Family and Community in the Slave South.* New York: Oxford University Press, 1996.

Wolf, Stephanie Grauman. *As Various as Their Land: The Everyday Lives of Eighteenth-Century Americans.* New York: Harper Collins, 1993.

Wood, Gordon S. "Patriarchal Dependence" and "Enlightened Paternalism." In *The Radicalism of the American Revolution.* New York: Alfred A. Knopf, 1991.

Yentsch, Anne Elizabeth. "The Face of Urban Slavery." Chap. 9 in *A Chesapeake Family and Their Slaves: A Study in Historical Archaeology.* Cambridge: Cambridge University Press, 1994.

Virginia's House of Burgesses was determined to protect its exclusive right to tax the colony.

CHOOSING REVOLUTION

Detail from *The Death of General Warren at the Battle of Bunker's Hill,* by John Trumbull, oil on canvas, England, 1786. Courtesy, Yale University Art Gallery, New Haven, Conn.

CHOOSING REVOLUTION

The "Choosing Revolution" story line traces the beginnings of the new nation by exploring the complex decisions every Virginian faced as the colony moved toward independence.

KEY POINTS

- BACKGROUND. The "Choosing Revolution" story line focuses primarily on choice, but choice must be defined more broadly than just the single choice for or against armed rebellion. An individual's decision to choose, or not choose, revolution was based on a series of choices over the fifteen to twenty years before the battle of Yorktown. During those years, Virginians reacted to issues arising from the Seven Years' War, the Stamp Act, internal crises like the Robinson Affair in 1766, the Townshend Duties, nonimportation associations, the Gunpowder Incident, the forming of a new government, and the mobilization and support of the American army. As they considered their ideas about natural rights and government, as well as their life circumstances and the events around them, many Virginians made a commitment to freedom, liberty, and popular sovereignty.

- THE CONTENDERS. Backed by Parliament, the British ministry sought active management of a widespread empire in the aftermath of the Seven Years' War. At the same time, Virginia's political leaders in the General Assembly determined to protect their prerogative to draft legislation for the colony.

- THE BRITISH CONSTITUTION. Under the British constitutional settlement of 1688, supreme authority rested with Parliament, where royalty, nobility, and the commons were all represented. Liberty was the power to act freely within laws enacted fairly by a balance of these three interests.

- UNFAIR LEGISLATION. By the 1760s, many Americans and Britons perceived that ministerial corruption and the buying of Parliamentary elections breached the integrity of the commons and resulted in unfairly enacted laws that were a threat to traditional British liberty. Americans began to doubt whether the British constitution could adequately protect their natural rights, including personal security, personal liberty, and private property.

- VIRGINIA POLITICS. The younger, more aggressive leaders urged a forceful protest against British policies, but this was possible only with the support of the yeomanry. Increasingly diverse in ethnicity and religion,

Visual symbols played an important role in defining patriotism and power. The royal images of the British coat of arms and King George III were replaced by new national images of the eagle and George Washington.

The British coat of arms from a painting of a type intended for courthouses and other public buildings *(above top)*.

The American eagle. Patriotic symbols became popular decorations for home furnishings in America *(above bottom)*.

George the Third, attributed to the school of Allan Ramsay, oil on canvas, Great Britain, 1761–1770 *(above middle)*.

George Washington, by Charles Willson Peale, oil on canvas, Philadelphia, 1780 *(above right)*.

the yeomanry responded when the gentry leadership invoked property ownership as a common economic interest between the two groups and became increasingly active politically.

- CHOOSING SIDES.   Whites of all social ranks, free blacks, slaves, and Native Americans considered both ideology and self-interest as they chose, or did not choose, revolution.

- THE STORY CONTINUES.   The war years transformed the political rhetoric of protest into the political principles that guided nation building, including conflicting imperatives to honor individual liberty and uphold the public good.

- PROPERTY OWNERSHIP.   The Virginia elite's efforts to ally their interests with the yeomanry had far-reaching consequences. Their promotion of property ownership as almost a sacred right protected the institution of slavery. Some sought common ground with the yeomanry by portraying African-Americans as inferior to whites and as a potentially explosive element in society. These attitudes continue to reverberate today.

- WRITTEN CONSTITUTION.   Our written constitution is a legacy of the Revolution. By means of the form of government it established, we continue to balance individual liberty against the public good as each issue arises. Through these channels of government, we continue to extend full rights to groups within our society who have not had them before as we redefine the reality of our liberty, freedom, and equality.

BACKGROUND AND THESIS

Classes and textbooks about American history have helped to familiarize visitors with the "Choosing Revolution" story. At Colonial Williamsburg, they will discover how eighteenth-century Virginians—great and small, black and white, men and women, patriots and loyalists—perceived the events that led to the American Revolution.

When Richard Bland and other political leaders began to express concern about imperial policies in the early 1760s, none could yet imagine a separate nation. Nor did they regard themselves as revolutionaries. As the debate continued, however, ideas derived from the British constitutional settlement of 1688 began to evolve into a distinctly American political philosophy based on freedom, liberty, and popular sovereignty. Eventually, many free Virginians came to believe that separation from Great Britain was preferable to remaining a colony. Others took alternate paths. Loyalists believed in many of the principles that patriots espoused, which they fulfilled by pledging their allegiance to the Crown. Slaves who fled to the British army were expressing their desire for freedom although their rebellion was against Virginia masters, not royal authority. A number of colonial Virginians sat out the war, never committing themselves to one political principle or another. Equivocation was their strategy for surviving the turmoil of the times.

Many complicated choices, none clearly right or wrong, make up the "Choosing Revolution" story line.

THE CONTENDERS

Two contending groups figured prominently in these events. The British ministry sought actively to manage the vast empire that Britain had acquired after the Seven Years' War. The ministers' policies often came into conflict with those of powerful political leaders in the Virginia General Assembly who were determined to protect their prerogative to write legislation for the colony. Although Virginia's leaders were generally united on the basic issues after 1765, they were divided over the best course to follow. Younger, more aggressive leaders including Patrick Henry advocated direct protests, while conservative, "responsible" elders headed by Peyton Randolph counseled moderation. Henry and his supporters were scorned as the "popular" faction because they sought to make common cause with the yeomanry. The hotheads argued that the British government's assault on the gentry's autonomy in enacting legislation endangered the interests of the middling sorts as well.

Patrick Henry, by Thomas Sully, oil on canvas, America, 1815.

Peyton Randolph, photographic reproduction. Courtesy, Virginia Historical Society, Richmond, Va.

THE BRITISH CONSTITUTION

The British constitution was not a written document but rather an accepted set of principles that had evolved from precedent and experience. Britain's laws and institutions were based on moral rights, reason, and justice. Promoting the public good was the ultimate goal. Ideally, the British constitution maintained a balance between royalty, nobility, and commons, the three orders of society. Royalty represented monarchy, which unchecked could degenerate into tyranny; the nobility represented aristocracy, which always threatened to become an oligarchy; and the commons represented democracy, which, left unrestrained, tended toward mob rule.

As long as each order protected its own sphere against encroachment by the other two, the rights of all were assured. The constitutional settlement of 1688 invested supreme authority (sovereignty) in Parliament where all three orders were represented. Liberty was perceived as the power to act freely within a system of laws enacted fairly by a balance of the three interests.

In the 1760s, Americans began to express the opinion that the colonies preserved British liberties better than the mother country did. They warned that ministerial corruption and the buying of Parliamentary elections had compromised the integrity of the commons and resulted in unfairly enacted laws that were a threat to liberty. In this atmosphere of political uncertainty, Virginians agreed with the many Americans who feared that their natural rights, including personal security, personal liberty, and private property, were endangered by the shift in government policy that followed the Seven Years' War.

Little by little, Americans started to question whether the constitution was strong enough to safeguard British liberties when reason and justice, the guiding principles essential to it, were superseded by corruption. Americans also began to doubt that an unwritten constitution, which could easily be altered by circumstances, afforded adequate protection of their rights. Some argued the ideal constitution should be a written document that defined the form of government and determined how its authority was to be shared among its branches. For example, they held that the legislature should derive its power from the constitution, not the other way around as in British practice. The best constitution would not *grant* rights but would *guarantee* the natural rights men possessed. Thus, new American—and new Virginian—political principles emerged partly as a result of the contest of wills between Virginia leaders and British officials. The dialogue between members of Virginia's General Assembly and their constituents also helped to shape the new philosophy of government.

A View of the House of Commons, by B. Cole, black and white line engraving, England, ca. 1755. Parliament had been the trustee of the unwritten English constitution that protected the rights of Englishmen since 1688. By the 1760s, American colonists felt that Parliament had become corrupt and believed that the preservation of English liberties now rested with their own governments.

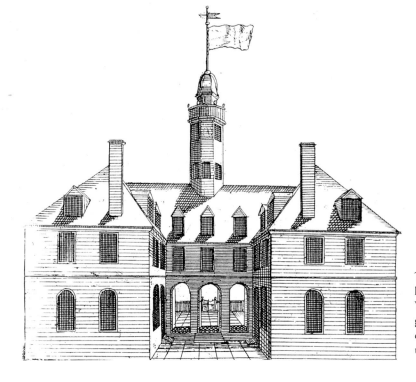

The Capitol in Williamsburg housed the government of Virginia. The House of Burgesses was the site of many key decisions in the move toward independence.

Thomas Jefferson, by Gilbert Stuart, oil on canvas, America, ca. 1805.

VIRGINIA POLITICS

Since the late seventeenth century, Virginia's political leaders had maintained their control of society by persuading middling planters that they shared a common set of values grounded in social deference, familial patriarchy, marketplace patronage, and slavery. As the yeomanry became increasingly diversified in both ethnic origin and religious persuasion, the alliance began to unravel in the 1760s. Spokesmen for the upper classes responded by emphasizing that ownership of property was the crucial element uniting gentry and freeholder interests. The gentry warned that if Virginians permitted Parliament to impose taxation without representation, they would be regarded as little better than slaves themselves. No white property-owning Virginian could misunderstand the threat. Property owners were determined to continue to identify themselves as not slaves; in doing so, they perpetuated the social chasm between whites and blacks.

This appeal to shared economic interests and the political discourse that followed from it revealed that the political system in Virginia diverged from the British model in significant respects. Unencumbered by the restraints of an inherited hierarchy, new economic and social opportunities in Virginia encouraged ambitious individuals to advance their self-interest regardless of their background. Since free Virginians had greater access to land than did their British counterparts, more men were enfranchised in the colony than in the mother country. The frequently repeated gentry claim that the elected General Assembly in Virginia represented the "people's interests" rang true, especially in contrast to the corrupt, interest-ridden British Parliament. In July 1774, Williamsburg voters eliminated the traditional election practice (which was based on British precedent) of "treating" the voters. Their repre-

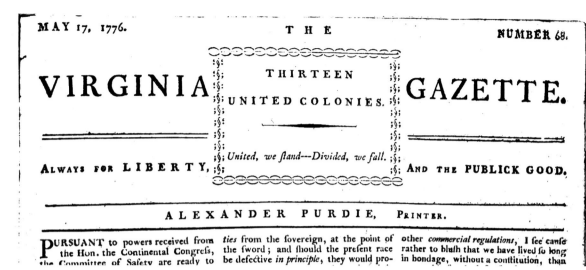

MAY 17, 1776.   THE   NUMBER 68.

VIRGINIA THIRTEEN UNITED COLONIES. GAZETTE.

United, we stand---Divided, we fall.

ALWAYS FOR LIBERTY,   AND THE PUBLICK GOOD.

ALEXANDER PURDIE, PRINTER.

PURSUANT to powers received from the Hon. the Continental Congress, the Committee of Safety are ready to | ties from the sovereign, at the point of the sword; and should the present race be defective *in principle*, they would pro- | other *commercial regulations*, I see cause rather to blush that we have lived so long in bondage, without a constitution, than

As tensions increased, Virginians began to choose between loyalty to the Crown or to the colony. In May 1776, Alexander Purdie, printer of the *Virginia Gazette,* publicly announced the choice of a united thirteen colonies by creating a new masthead for his newspaper.

sentative was instructed to forego the ritual lest it taint the forthcoming election by implying that the suffrage of free men could be bought for a few cups of bumbo. For gentry and yeomanry alike, portraying Virginia as a freehold republic legitimated the concept of separation from the mother country and made it appear virtuous. When Virginians codified their newly forged principles in the "Declaration of Rights," the pursuit of independence became an act of moral rectitude.

To dare to imagine a nation independent from Great Britain, Virginians first had to believe themselves capable of self-government. The systems of local and provincial governance that had been evolving in colonial Virginia strengthened their conviction that they were ready. Gentry control of local institutions, especially county courts and vestries, led to dominance in provincial affairs. During the decades before the Revolution, the House of Burgesses had consolidated its power at the expense of the royal governor's.

As the political leadership concentrated power in its own hands, grassroots politics had begun to shift toward a more popular style. Virginia's newspapers helped create a public political forum shared by literate yeomen and gentry. Newspapers were circulated and discussed in taverns, stores, and other informal meeting places, linking a widely separated readership and fostering the development of a better informed citizenry.

The House of Burgesses, at the center of events between 1765 and 1776, came to represent the ideal of self-government for all free Virginians. The importance of the assembly as the "people's forum" was underscored in 1775 and 1776 when, as the imperial crisis worsened, yeomen voters, flexing their new civic muscle, instructed their elected burgesses how to vote. On April 24, 1776, the James City County freeholders, meeting at Allen's Ordinary outside Williamsburg, declared that the time had come for the colonies to sever their connection with Great Britain. They ordered their representatives to the

Fifth Virginia Convention, William Norvell and Robert Carter Nicholas, to exert their "utmost" abilities to see that this action was taken.

Restrictions on the settlement of the frontier after the Seven Years' War had struck at the heart of Virginians' hopes for economic and social advancement. Small planters experienced increasing difficulties in obtaining land, a development that only enhanced their aspirations to become landowners, and they were determined to acquire the status that owning property would endow. Although Virginia society had become highly stratified on the eve of the Revolution, social advancement was possible as long as land continued to be available. Virginians reaffirmed their belief in the primacy of landowner-ship in the Declaration of Rights, which proclaimed that all men were en-titled to the "enjoyment of Life and liberty with the means of acquiring and possessing property."

But all men and women were not thought to be equally free. Virginians lived uneasily with the paradox of celebrating freedom while condoning slav-ery. Political rhetoric defending personal freedom was belied by the reality of two hundred thousand enslaved blacks who were denied the most basic liber-ties. The same rhetoric that defended private property, thereby giving official sanction to racism, prevented colonists who were troubled by the contradic-tion between principle and practice from responding effectively. Fear also blocked reform. Virginians feared slave insurrections; they also envisioned social chaos, economic disruption, and loss of property should slavery end. Governor Dunmore played on these anxieties when he summoned Virginia slaves to join the British cause against the rebel slave masters. In the end, the paradox of slavery was simply acknowledged and removed from political dis-course.

The able Doctor, or America Swallowing the Bitter Draught, maker unknown, black and white line engrav-ing, England, 1774. This print appeared soon after the Boston Tea Party. It shows Lord North, the British Prime Minister, forcing tea down the throat of America.

Hamilton delin.   Noble scalp.

*The Manner in which the American Colonies Declared themselves Independant of the King of England, throughout
the different Provinces, on July 4, 1776,* by George Noble from a drawing of William Hamilton, black and white
line engraving, England, 1783.

The Death of General Warren at the Battle of Bunker's Hill, by John Trumbull, oil on canvas, England, 1786. Courtesy, Yale University Art Gallery, New Haven, Conn.

CHOOSING SIDES

Going to war against Great Britain was a bold—some said a suicidal—act. The decision stands as a defining moment in the "Becoming Americans" story just as it was for every man, woman, and child—slave or free—in Virginia. Once war was declared, individuals made responsible, expedient, considered choices as they took the measure of their political loyalties or declined to do so, preparing to hedge their bets. Some Virginia loyalists such as John Randolph believed that war with the mother country was such a reckless, misguided course of action that they exiled themselves to England rather than participate. Others chose to remain in Virginia, where they suffered hardships and persecution for their devotion to Great Britain. James Innes, usher at the college, became captain of the Williamsburg company of volunteers. Edward Digges of Williamsburg left the college before he was sixteen to join the fight for independence.

A significant number chose to defer a decision until the military success of one side or another seemed assured or until local pressure made further indecision impossible. A few, like Williamsburg printer William Hunter and lawyer James Hubard, switched sides. In most cases, dependent family mem-

Detail from *The Death of Major Pierson,* by John Singleton Copley, oil on canvas, England, 1783. Courtesy, Tate Gallery, London.

STAFFORD county, AQUIA, *Nov* 8, 1775.
RUN off laſt night from the ſubſcriber, a negro man named CHARLES, who is a very ſhrewd ſenſible fellow, and can both read and write; and as he has always waited upon me, he muſt be well known through moſt parts of *Virginia* and *Maryland.* He is very black, has a large noſe, and is about 5 feet 8 or 10 inches high. He took a variety of clothes, which I cannot well particulariſe, ſtole ſeveral of my ſhirts, a pair of new ſaddle bags, and two mares, one a darkiſh, the other a light bay, with a blaze and white feet, and about 3 years old. From many circumſtances, there is reaſon to believe he intends an attempt to get to lord *Dunmore;* and as I have reaſon to believe his deſign of going off was long premeditated, and that he has gone off with ſome accomplice, I am apprehenſive he may prove daring and reſolute, if endeavoured to be taken. His elopement was from no cauſe of complaint, or dread of a whipping (for he has always been remarkably indulged, indeed too much ſo) but from a determined reſolution to get liberty, as he conceived, by flying to lord *Dunmore.* I will give 5l. to any perſon who ſecures him, and the mares, ſo that I get them again.
ROBERT BRENT.
N. B. Since writing the above advertiſement, the mares have returned, and there is a great probability, from many

Slaves fought on both sides during the Revolutionary War. The owner of Charles, a runaway slave who had a "determined resolution to get liberty" promised by the British to slaves who fought on their side, offered a reward for his return in the *Virginia Gazette.*

bers followed the choice of the head of the household (whether man or woman), sharing in the consequences willy-nilly. Occasionally, sons or slaves made opposite choices. Edmund Randolph did not share his father's loyalty to the king's cause and remained in America as an aide-de-camp to General Washington. Slaves from several Williamsburg households, including the Cockes' and the McClurgs', defected to the British army in 1781.

Economics as well as ideology figured in the choice for or against revolution. Merchants dependent on commerce with Great Britain stood to lose by both economic boycotts and by war. For example, milliner Catherine Rathell closed her business and boarded a ship for Great Britain. By contrast, tradesmen who produced the matériel of war expected to prosper from a conflict. James Anderson, blacksmith, and Peter Powell, wheelwright, expanded their operations to supply the American army.

Native Americans also chose sides during the war, basing their decisions on the outcome they believed would serve their group's interest. Many hoped that the conflict between the British and Americans would enable them to regain some ground they had lost to the whites. In 1775, Dunmore tried unsuccessfully to combine Native Americans with British forces to cut Virginia off from the northern colonies, a move that further inflamed anti-

The Alternative of Williams-burg, attributed to Philip Dawe, black and white mezzotint engraving, England, 1775. Virginia loyalists are being forced to sign a nonimportation agreement. The alternative was tarring and feathering.

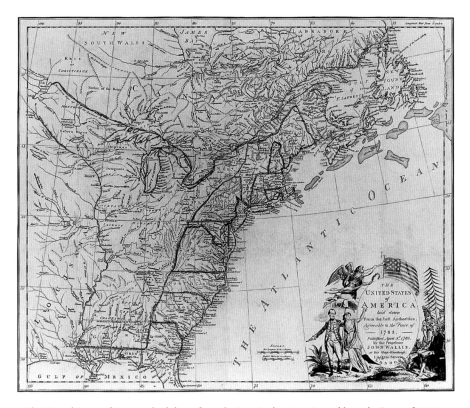

The United States of America laid down from the Best Authorities, Agreeable to the Peace of 1783, published by John Wallis, line engraving, London, 1783. This map shows the state boundaries and Indian lands of the new nation. It was published five months before Great Britain and the United States signed the definitive treaty of peace that ended the American Revolution.

British sentiments in the colony. To the north, British Major Henry Hamilton allied with Indians to harass the frontier. Ultimately, the Americans captured Hamilton and brought him to the public gaol in Williamsburg.

British and American forces sometimes committed atrocities against one other's Indian allies, causing the Indians to change sides. The Cherokees, supported by the British, attacked the southern frontier, but when their towns were ravaged by the Americans, they sued for peace. After a preliminary treaty had been negotiated, forty Cherokee men and women came to Williamsburg in 1777 on a goodwill visit.

George Rogers Clark and his relatively few troops kept the British and Indians sufficiently occupied so that American armies in the East were not needed in the West. Neither British nor Americans won a decisive victory in the West, and the Native Americans obtained no permanent advantage from their participation. The Cherokees, in fact, were forced to negotiate away even more land.

CONCLUSION

Every Virginian knew that if the patriots prevailed, thirteen separate colonies would form a new, independent nation. Victory would turn rebellion into revolution. The war years transformed the political rhetoric of protest into the political philosophy that later guided nation building. It left unresolved the irreconcilable tension between individual liberty and the public good, the twin promises of freedom and equality. What emerged in Virginia was a society dedicated to widespread property ownership among free whites. Their access to land gave rise to the fundamental belief that, despite great disparities in wealth and reputation, America was "the best poor man's country" where hard work and enterprise could produce a "decent competence."

The balance between individual liberty and the general welfare remains unresolved in American society. It never can be. Each generation emphasizes one or the other as new issues arise, usually through legislation or judicial review. Each reinterpretation reopens the ancient contest, as the current debates about both freedom of religion and freedom of expression illustrate. These issues push roots deep into the soil of revolutionary ideals. The issue of use of private property versus environmental protection has its origins in revolutionary ideas about the inviolability of private ownership in the land of opportunity on one hand, and the greater good of all on the other.

The efforts of Virginia gentlemen to make common cause with the yeomanry produced far-reaching consequences. The gentry's promotion of property ownership almost as a sacred right ultimately protected the practice of slavery. Belief in the sanctity of property posed an unsolvable dilemma for many revolutionary Virginians. They knew that slavery was wrong, but they also believed that legislation to free slaves without just compensation to the slaves' owners would be tantamount to confiscation and, therefore, equally wrong. Other Virginians whose self-interest embraced slave ownership defended slavery as compatible with democratic republican ideals by citing the example of ancient Rome. They argued that any group of people who could be bent to the will of another was unworthy of citizenship in a republic. This definition included the poor and dependent. And who was poorer or more dependent than a slave? They concluded that the preservation of the republic ultimately protected the poor and dependent.

This line of reasoning forestalled any serious abolition movement in Virginia. It later became a keystone in Virginians' definition of republicanism. Further, to cement their alliance with the yeomanry, some wealthy landowners deliberately preyed on the fears and prejudices that most whites harbored about African-Americans. This racist view of blacks as inferior to whites and as a potentially explosive element in society kept them disenfranchised well into the twentieth century. It continues to reverberate in contemporary society.

A country born of an armed rebellion finds itself in a quandary. Obliged to legitimize its origins, the government must discourage and suppress later factions who raise the banner of civil war. From the Whiskey Rebellion, through the Civil War, to modern "militia groups," some dissenters in our society have used the American Revolution to justify violent rebellion against the federal government.

Most changes in society have been channeled through the institutions of government that our written constitution established after the Revolutionary War. Even so, social change has often been slow in coming. The franchise and equal treatment under the law have been extended to women, racial and ethnic minorities, immigrants, and children only in the twentieth century. Some groups still seek freedom from discrimination. As Americans, we struggle ceaselessly to redefine the reality of liberty, freedom, and equality.

"CHOOSING REVOLUTION" AND THE "BECOMING AMERICANS" THEME

DIVERSE PEOPLES

People of many cultures and beliefs came together in Revolutionary Virginia. The colony's populace consisted of English, Scots, Irish, Welsh, Africans and African-Americans, Native Americans, Germans, and others. Growing numbers of religious dissenters held ideas that departed from those of the established church. Of these many peoples, some were American patriots, some were loyalists, and some switched sides or remained uncommitted. Loyalists did not always agree among themselves about their priorities or the best course of action to take. Nor did patriots. For example, within the ranks of Virginia's leadership a "generation gap" pitted the older conservatives against the younger "hotheads."

CLASHING INTERESTS

The most obvious clash of viewpoints in the "Choosing Revolution" story line was between British and American interests. The British government's ideas about managing the colonies conflicted with some Americans' ideas about liberty and their rights as citizens. Virginians had to sort out where their loyalties lay.

In addition to revolutionary politics, there were other grounds for dissension within Virginia. European and Native American beliefs about land and ownership differed. The interests of the Virginia yeomanry and the gentlemen freeholders were often in conflict. Planters flooding into Southside Virginia faced different economic needs than Tidewater planters. Germans and Ulster Scots settling the backcountry brought different ethnic values with them. Growing numbers of religious dissenters in the 1760s and 1770s openly condemned the dissipation and extravagance of gentry culture. The slaves' desire for personal freedom and white people's perception of slaves as chattel property produced conflicts of interest that could not be resolved.

SHARED VALUES

Virginians shared a reverence for liberty and natural rights, although they did not always agree about the best means of securing them. Some clung to the British constitution, which had long safeguarded the British heritage of liberty. Others looked to new political ideas that emphasized popular sovereignty. Slaves could enjoy liberty only by joining the military or running away.

The colony's most powerful gentlemen emphasized property ownership as the fundamental link between themselves and the yeomanry, enabling them to make common cause against British policies that assailed property rights and diminished opportunities to acquire land. Land was a symbol of social and economic advancement for all whites. Emphasis on property further solidified the institution of slavery, as did the shared racial prejudice of most white Virginians.

FORMATIVE INSTITUTIONS

The hint that their interests mattered politically encouraged yeomen to participate actively in the public political forum. Newspapers allowed them to share their views in a common, broadly based, political discourse. Extra-legal countywide meetings of freeholders presented immediate opportunities for yeoman participation and influence. The House of Burgesses became increasingly important as a forum in which representatives of the people could voice their concerns.

PARTIAL FREEDOMS

White male property holders who espoused the revolutionary cause enjoyed the lion's share of privileges in Virginia because they were the voters and officeholders. Just before and during the Revolutionary War, many Virginians became increasingly intolerant of dissenting political viewpoints and sought to forge a consensus by exercising the power of the majority. Those who could not bring themselves to accept the patriots' position suffered accordingly. Some were forced into silence. Others were exiled and their property was confiscated. Also disadvantaged were those Virginians who were defined by political theorists of the day as undeserving of participation in civic society. Women, free African-Americans, and poor, propertyless white men were judged too dependent and too deficient in good sense to make the morally responsible decisions necessary to exercise the full rights of citizenship. Slaves who did not attain freedom by escape remained enmeshed in a system that treated them as property.

REVOLUTIONARY PROMISE

Before delegates to the fifth Virginia Convention adopted George Mason's draft of the Declaration of Rights, which declared "all men to be born equally free and independent," they added a clause stating that men were entitled to enjoy rights only "when they enter into a state of society." This addition made explicit the exclusionary principle that disenfranchised women and African-Americans until the twentieth century. The promises of freedom and equality remain elusive for some subcultures in American society even today.

CONNECTIONS TO OTHER "BECOMING AMERICANS" STORY LINES

TAKING POSSESSION

Imperial prohibitions against settlement west of the Alleghenies were little heeded by colonial Virginians who staked their fortunes and futures on western lands. A proportionally larger electorate in Virginia than in Great Britain reflected widespread landownership in the colony and allowed more political participation among the yeomanry. Individual choices for or against revolution were powerfully influenced by the promise and reality of owning land. Westward expansion also brought conflicts with Native Americans.

ENSLAVING VIRGINIA

Critics on both sides of the Atlantic were quick to point out the hypocrisy of white Virginians who insisted on their own liberty while denying it to slaves. Revolution nevertheless presented African-Americans with alternatives. Some chose loyalty to Britain as a path to freedom; others fought for the American cause.

REDEFINING FAMILY

The centuries-old image of the father as patriarch was gradually superseded during the eighteenth century by a new ideal that stressed greater freedom for family members who would be governed by affection. This important shift in family relationships carried a political message as well because it undercut one prop supporting monarchical authority.

As political protest evolved into war, women and children often acted as heads of households, running farms and businesses in the absence of husbands and fathers. The Revolution also divided families and disrupted family life. Choices split siblings and generations. Sometimes lesser family members were forced to accede to the preferences of the household head. Other times, members willfully severed familial ties. Sons made choices independent of and different from their fathers'. Slaves who ran away from their white masters often left their own kin behind.

BUYING RESPECTABILITY

Virginia's leaders shrewdly calculated the importance of the consumer market when they planned the boycotts of British goods. High demand for manufactured and imported goods was a consequence of an expanding middle-class market for commodities once thought appropriate only for the gentry. Americans in every colony shared the consumer experience, so taxes on imported goods led disenchanted colonists to regard themselves as common victims of British tyranny. Consumer goods became potent political symbols. Nonimportation associations that emphasized local manufactures brought about changes in the household economy, including the production of cloth by women.

FREEING RELIGION

Religious dissenters after mid-century resented laws mandating state support for the Anglican church. Their grievances opened a dialogue that eventually led to its disestablishment. Evangelicals who decried the immorality of the social and ecclesiastical elite in Virginia prepared listeners for the revolutionary rhetoric that contrasted English corruption with American virtue. The evangelicals influenced the new political style that celebrated common people gathered together in popular assemblies.

Story Line Team: Bill White, Harvey Bakari, Carol Dozier, Jan Gilliam, Tom Hay, Cathy Hellier, Russ Lawson, Nancy Milton, and Ken Schwarz.

FURTHER READING

Anderson, Fred. *The Crucible of War: The Seven Years' War and the Fate of Empire in British North America, 1754–1766.* New York: Alfred A. Knopf, 2002.

Bailyn, Bernard. *The Ideological Origins of the American Revolution.* Cambridge, Mass.: Harvard University Press, 1967.

Billings, Warren M., John E. Selby, and Thad W. Tate. *Colonial Virginia: A History.* New York: KTD, 1986.

Frey, Sylvia R. *Water from the Rock: Black Resistance in a Revolutionary Age.* Princeton, N. J.: Princeton University Press, 1991.

Greene, Jack P. *Negotiated Authorities: Essays in Colonial Political and Constitutional History.* Charlottesville, Va.: University Press of Virginia, 1994.

Holton, Woody. *Forced Founders: Indians, Debtors, Slaves, and the Making of the American Revolution in Virginia.* Chapel Hill, N. C.: University of North Carolina Press, 1999.

Isaac, Rhys. *The Transformation of Virginia, 1740–1790.* Chapel Hill, N. C.: University of North Carolina Press, 1982.

Jefferson, Thomas. *Summary View of the Rights of British America.* Reprint. Delmar, N. Y.: Scholars' Facsimiles & Reprints, 1976.

Quarles, Benjamin. *The Negro in the American Revolution.* Chapel Hill, N. C.: University of North Carolina Press, 1961.

Selby, John E. *The Revolution in Virginia, 1775–1783.* Williamsburg, Va.: Colonial Williamsburg Foundation, 1988.

Sosin, Jack M. *The Revolutionary Frontier, 1763–1783.* New York: Holt, Rinehart and Winston, 1967.

Sydnor, Charles S. *American Revolutionaries in the Making: Political Practices in Washington's Virginia.* New York: Free Press, 1965. Formerly published in 1952 as *Gentlemen Freeholders: Political Practices in Washington's Virginia.*

Virginia Declaration of Rights. Text printed in *The George Mason Lectures, Honoring the Two Hundredth Anniversary of the Virginia Declaration of Rights.* Williamsburg, Va.: Colonial Williamsburg Foundation, 1976.

Wood, Gordon S. *The Radicalism of the American Revolution.* New York: Alfred A. Knopf, 1992.

Wood, Peter H. "'Liberty is Sweet': African-American Struggles in the Years before White Independence." In *Beyond the American Revolution: Explorations in the History of American Radicalism.* Edited by Alfred F. Young. DeKalb, Ill.: Northern Illinois University Press, 1993.

America Triumphant and Britannia in Distress, maker unknown, black and white etching, Boston, 1782.
The etching, one of only a few political prints that appeared in American publications, celebrates America's independence. The flag is an early representation of the stars and stripes.

Colonial Virginians from all ranks and cultural traditions had a religious world view.

FREEING RELIGION

First Anglican Communion at Jamestown, June 21, 1607, bas-relief. Courtesy, Cook Collection, Valentine Museum, Richmond, Va. One of the colonists' missions was to carry Protestant Christianity to the native peoples they encountered in Virginia.

FREEING RELIGION

The "Freeing Religion" story line surveys religious life in colonial Virginia and explains how Native American, African, and European religions in the colony were shaped by the legally sanctioned Church of England, by the evangelical movement that inspired many Virginians to abandon the established church for dissenting sects, and by the philosophical, political, and social changes that culminated in the passage of a law guaranteeing the free exercise of religion.

KEY POINTS

- PERVASIVE PRESENCE. Religion permeated everyday life and learning in eighteenth-century Virginia.

- STATE CHURCH. Established and protected by law, the Church of England was the predominant religious institution in the Virginia colony.

- SEPARATION OF CHURCH AND STATE. As many Virginians responded to the appeal of evangelical faith and the tolerant rationalism of the Enlightenment, they moved away from the idea of a single authoritarian church protected by the state and toward the concept of religion disassociated from government.

- CRADLE OF LIBERTY. The personal appeal of evangelical faith and the ideals of the Enlightenment helped create an atmosphere in which democratic ideas developed.

- EQUAL BEFORE GOD. As Evangelical Christianity's message of equality before God filtered through African-American culture, it merged with Old Testament images of deliverance to give many slaves a heightened sense of spiritual identity and new inner strength for resisting slavery.

- UNWILLING SUBJECTS. Native Americans' reluctance to convert to Christianity and adopt other English customs encouraged land-hungry colonists and British officials to conclude that encroachment on Indian lands and the near-extermination of native populations were justified.

Background and Thesis

The first colonists knelt in a prayer of thanksgiving when they arrived on the shores of Virginia in 1607. The Protestant Church of England that prescribed the order of service they followed was not yet seventy-five years old. Henry VIII (1491–1547) broke with the Roman Catholic Church in the 1530s to make himself—not the Pope—head of the English church. Henry's action made the English church independent of Rome, but Protestant reform was a restrained and lengthy process in England.

Devotional practice and liturgy under Henry retained a rich medieval Catholic framework. During Edward VI's few years on the throne (1547–1553), the church bore the imprint of the king's Protestant tutors and advisers: worship services were conducted in English, the Mass was downplayed and divested of some of its mystery, and churches were stripped of religious images. Mary Tudor (1553–1558) forced the church back into the Catholic fold with considerable support from the laity before Elizabeth I (1553–1603) and her bishops took a "middle way" in order to accommodate a wide spectrum of Protestant opinion—from high church Anglicans who favored ritualistic worship to low church reformers who tolerated bishops and other holdovers from medieval Catholicism. Nonetheless, the "Elizabethan settlement" left two groups outside the Church of England: intractable Catholics, who refused to forswear their allegiance to the Pope, and extreme Protestants (Puritans) influenced by Calvinism, who believed the vestiges of Latin liturgy in Anglican services and the church's episcopal organization were contrary to scripture.

In the next century, the religion—Catholic or Protestant—of rulers in most Christian countries dictated the religion of their subjects as it had for hundreds of years. State churches were believed to reinforce the power of government. In turn, laws protected "established" churches and safeguarded orthodoxy by suppressing or limiting dissent, while public taxes defrayed church expenses.

In England, Anglican bishops (with royal approval) eventually agreed on thirty-nine articles of faith "for avoiding of Diversities of Opinion, and for the stablishing [sic] of Consent touching True Religion." The deliberately ambiguous language in these articles allowed for considerable variation in personal beliefs. Protestants generally depended less on church tradition for religious authority and more on the Bible for God's truth, however. Dissent from Anglicanism was inevitable as reformers interpreted scripture for themselves. Parliament permitted dissenters to assemble legally for worship provided they followed the rules set forth in the Act of Toleration of 1689. Nonetheless, they could not hold public office or avoid paying taxes to the Church of England.

Scattered settlement during the first century of colonization and the absence of a church hierarchy headed by a bishop forced changes in the established Church of England in Virginia. For instance, parish vestries composed of laymen took control of church affairs in the colony. Dissenters from the Anglican church enjoyed broad religious toleration up to the middle of the eighteenth century. After the Virginia Convention adopted the Declaration of Rights in June 1776, evangelical dissenters joined forces with political leaders influenced by the tolerant rationalism of the Enlightenment to expand free exercise of religion, while Anglicans who clung to the idea of centralized church authority tried to limit it.

Ten years after the outbreak of the Revolution, Virginians were in the vanguard of American constitutional change when they broke with nearly fifteen hundred years of Christian tradition by cutting the ties that bound the Anglican church in Virginia to the state. In the process, they freed themselves to worship under whatever religious roof they preferred or never to darken a church door at all.

WORLD VIEWS AT ODDS

English-speaking whites, Native Americans, and Africans, the three main groups who interacted in Virginia, operated within prescientific belief systems that included supreme beings, a variety of lesser benevolent entities, troublesome spirits and devils, explanations of good and evil, and stories about creation and the afterlife. In the colonial period, traditional religions of Indians and Africans came under intense pressure from the dominant Anglo-Virginian culture.

Besides envisioning opportunities for commercial gain, the king, Virginia Company investors, and colonists also regarded the Virginia experiment as a noble effort to fulfill the biblical injunction "Go ye therefore, and teach all nations, baptizing them in the name of the Father, and of the Son, and of the Holy Ghost" by converting Indians to their Christian God. Christianity and civilization were nearly synonymous in Tudor-Stuart England. This was reflected in the English social order where human beings occupied positions of increasing importance and responsibility in an ascending hierarchy from the lowliest servant or slave to the monarch. English colonists in Virginia were therefore confident their god intended for them to impose an "orderly government," not the Christian religion alone, on the non-Christian peoples they encountered.

The Anglo-Virginians expected to convert the fifteen to twenty thousand Algonquian-speaking native inhabitants (Powhatans) of the Tsenacomoco coastal plain. The Powhatans were polytheistic, and their priests interceded with several deities to bring rain and cure disease. Powhatans were mindful of the remote Ahone, a beneficent god, but the most important deity in their

Indians dancing, by John White, watercolor drawing, 1585. Courtesy, Trustees of the British Museum, London.
Native Americans in Virginia already had well-developed traditional religions.

pantheon was the guardian Okeus who, if not properly appeased, visited sickness, crop failure, or other catastrophes on those who offended him. Traditional beliefs bound tribal members to each other and to the natural world in an ethos that English settlers and Virginia-born colonists could not fathom or take seriously. This cultural blindness was evident when Indian agent Robert Beverley and a party of his companions rifled a Powhatan temple toward the end of the seventeenth century without recognizing that their investigation was an act of desecration. In turn, most Native Americans spurned the monotheistic religion of the English invaders.

Most West Africans transported to Virginia had been brought up in complex belief systems distinguished by close relationships between the natural world and the supernatural, the secular and the sacred. West Africans considered God to be omniscient and omnipotent. Their knowledge and worship of God was expressed in songs, names, myths, religious ceremonies, prayers, and proverbs. Supreme or creator gods such as Onyame, Mawu, and Olorun had only a remote connection to people's daily lives. Worshipers were most attentive to an array of lesser divinities, personages, and intermediaries associated with the forces of nature such as Oya in the Yoruba country, who was goddess of the Niger River and wife of Shango the thunder god, and Olokun, who owned the sea in Yoruba, Bini, and Ibo.

The Yoruba recognized more than seventeen hundred divinities known collectively as Orisa, and the Ashanti worshiped many divinities known as the Abosom whom God had created to guard and protect men, whereas most African societies revered one or two. Orisa incorporated Ogun, the god of iron and steel, and Orunmila, who understood "every language spoken on earth," for example. These sky, earth, water, and forest spirits paid close attention to the concerns of humans. Eshu, a trickster god in Dahomey and Nigeria, could bring evil on a house, although he was not purely satanic since daily propitiation garnered his protection and favor. Africans torn from the supportive embrace of these belief systems were hard put to reestablish them on Virginia plantations where slaves from different regions of Africa were thrown together without common language or customs and where slave owners dismissed or forbade what to them were "outlandish" or dangerous practices.

Challenges to personal and institutional religion in the eighteenth century also came from the far-reaching effects of two important movements, the Enlightenment and the Great Awakening. Expanding scientific and philosophical horizons encouraged educated people to esteem science as the conqueror of superstition and ignorance. Enlightened thought inevitably led them to question accepted Christian truths based on biblical revelation. Intellectual rumination on the nature of God was very different from the emotional Bible-based religion that spread through Virginia during the series of revivals known as the Great Awakening in the late 1730s and '40s. Virginians from all walks of life embraced the message delivered by evangelical preachers who emphasized immediate personal understanding of religious truth through the joyful acceptance of a gospel of repentance and redemption.

ANGLICAN VIRGINIA

The Anglican church establishment was well organized by 1725. All but a few parishes had ministers, in marked contrast to the severe shortage of clergy in the previous century. New church buildings that dotted the landscape featured raised pulpits, communion tables accessible to the congregation, monarchical arms, and ranked seating, all of which reflected Protestant reforms and reinforced the social hierarchy.

The parish of Bruton erected its main church at Middle Plantation in 1684, although the settlement there was small and isolated. That church made Middle Plantation attractive to Commissary James Blair and Governor Francis Nicholson as the site for the college they hoped to found in the early 1690s. Bruton Parish Church and the College of William and Mary figured prominently in the decision to move the capital to Middle Plantation in 1699.

By that time, the Anglican clergy included an influential group of Scots in Anglican orders. One of them, James Blair, presided for fifty-four years over the church in Virginia as commissary, the Bishop of London' resident representative in Virginia. Blair founded the College of William and Mary including a divinity school to train clergymen from the colony. Blair's positions of commissary, president of the college, rector of Bruton Parish Church, and member of the governor's Council combined to lend considerable prestige to the established church, even though in practice his power over church matters and the Virginia clergy was quite limited.

No parish was without a minister by the late 1750s, and nearly one-third of the clergy were Virginia-born. Anglican ministers performed marriages, baptized infants and adults, taught the young, counseled the troubled, comforted the sick and bereaved, and buried the dead. After mid-century, the reputations of some Anglican parsons were seriously discredited as dissenters regularly admonished them for their worldliness and lack of spirituality. Modern historians frequently belittle the established clergy because of the misdeeds of a few corrupt parish priests. Most, however, were upright in their morals and respected by their parishioners.

Officeholders at all levels had to be members of the Anglican church. As a result, the overlapping jurisdictions of government and church concentrated political power in the hands of a relatively small group of Virginia leaders. The elite augmented their power by consolidating their control of colonial, county, and parish offices. In turn, the gentry, not an ecclesiastical hierarchy, imparted authority and standing to the established church.

An Anglican parish marked the area ministered to by a church and its vestry. It also served as a subdivision of the county for the administration of civil government. The vestry, a self-perpetuating panel of powerful laymen, met periodically to conduct church business, which included responsibilities that fall to secular authorities today. The vestry hired the parish minister when the governor failed to appoint one, kept a register of births and deaths in the parish, and levied taxes to fund construction and repair of church buildings, pay the minister's salary (set by law), and clean up church grounds. Vestrymen also spent tax monies to support indigent parishioners, and they placed poor orphans in the homes of craftsmen who agreed to teach them a trade. At the same time, county courts protected the estates of propertied orphans.

Virginia did not have church courts comparable to the ones in England, but county court justices exercised a combination of administrative, judicial, and ecclesiastical powers. Church officials and county justices cooperated to enforce laws governing moral conduct and religious obligations. Based in part on what churchwardens (two members of the vestry) told the county grand jury, justices exacted fines or imposed other punishments on offenders for bastardy, adultery, and too-frequent absence from Anglican church services.

Bruton Parish Church, by Francis Dayton, watercolor on paper, ca. 1950. Sunday services at Bruton Parish Church in Williamsburg provided opportunities for communal worship and social contact.

Coffeepot (both sides), earthenware (creamware), England, Staffordshire or York, ca. 1770. Inscriptions on this pot encouraged the hostess to keep her conversation "as becometh the gospel of Christ" and her company to remember the comforting words of the Twenty-third Psalm.

SPIRITUALITY AND COMMUNITY

In all likelihood, wealthy and middling Virginians shared the belief that religious sentiment ought to be nurtured within the framework of an organized church. Recent studies show that Anglican ministers frequently preached to full congregations on Sunday. Since gentry folk accounted for only a fraction of the population, small planters, merchants, artisans, and their families outnumbered the well-to-do in church. Every person (except formally declared dissenters) in eighteenth-century Virginia was a member of the Anglican church. As such, they were constrained by law to attend services at least once a month, although the courts enforced church attendance only sporadically.

Churchgoing had both spiritual and communal significance for Anglo-Virginians. Most Anglicans went to church regularly because religion gave them courage to face the uncertainties of everyday life and reinforced their understanding of their place in God's design. To be sure, colonial Anglicans eschewed outward displays of emotion or religious "enthusiasm." But they found confession, repentance, forgiveness, comfort, and unity in the familiar prayers and responses in the Book of Common Prayer, such as: "Almighty and most merciful Father; We have erred, and strayed from thy ways like lost sheep: We have followed too much the devices and desires of our own hearts: We have offended against thy holy laws; We have left undone those things which we ought to have done; And we have done those things which we ought not to have done; And there is no health in us."

Anglican ministers stressed moral instruction for Christian living in their sermons, thereby providing parishioners a standard against which to measure their personal behavior. William Byrd II wrote in his diaries of his remorse over repeated sins of the flesh. Gentlemen, it seems, subscribed to Christian ideals but did not always feel bound by them.

The once-a-week gatherings at the parish church were important social occasions. Before and after Sunday services, parishioners mingled with their neighbors, exchanging news of family and friends and making business and political contacts. Small planters, merchants, and craftsmen probably came to expect a certain civility and recognition from their "betters" in these church-yard exchanges.

Well-to-do families arrived and departed in coaches, humbler sorts in more practical wagons and carts, on horseback, or on foot. Seating patterns in Virginia Anglican churches "exhibited the community to itself in ranked order." Women and common planters were already in their seats when the gentlemen of the parish entered as a body. Ordered seating would have been especially evident in Williamsburg, where the elaborate box for the governor in Bruton Parish Church was in full view of the congregation.

Sundays in the eighteenth century found masters and their slaves at cross purposes. Slaves could attend church only if they obtained their master's consent. Moreover, white Virginians often invited friends and family home to dine after services, and slaves bore a large part of the workload on those occasions. Their duties took up some of the precious free time slaves had to visit their families and friends, hold their own religious meetings, and supplement their rations by raising chickens, growing vegetables, or trapping and fishing.

The religious lives of poor white parishioners and free blacks within the Anglican system remain obscure. During services, they probably occupied back benches in parish churches. Favored house slaves may have sat with their masters in family pews or boxes; others undoubtedly sat or stood in spaces on the periphery of the congregation. The formality and reserve of Anglican worship may not have appealed to these people as much as the emotionally charged meetings of evangelical sects, although Commissary Blair observed that many slaves attended Bruton Parish Church regularly and exhibited sincere religious feeling. Similarly, free blacks and other folk expressed their devotion to the Anglican way when they joined leading parishioners of Charles Parish, York County, in a petition to the General Assembly on behalf of the Protestant Episcopal Church in December 1786.

Slaves who worked in the master's household may have been permitted to sit in the family pew at the parish church.

Reflection on the minister's words, at least among the gentry, often took place within the family circle or in private meditations, as John Blair of Williamsburg recorded in his diary. Private libraries in Virginia contained Bibles and prayer books and more works on piety and morality than on any other subject. These included printed sermons, Bible commentaries, concordances, and devotional readings. The most popular—Bibles, prayer books, and *The Whole Duty of Man*—could also be found in non-gentry homes. Scriptural prints adorned the walls in many Virginia dwellings.

WOMEN IN THE ESTABLISHED CHURCH

Men of the Virginia gentry ran their parish churches, preached to congregations, openly displayed a Christian duty toward their fellows, and likely read prayers at home. Gentry women had no official duties in the Anglican church but were expected to live the Christian ideal. By the middle of the eighteenth century, women in well-to-do households took significant responsibility for their children's religious education. They exerted a strong influence on religious practices in their families. Betsy Randolph, Margaret Hornsby, and Anne Nicholas of Williamsburg and Lucy Nelson of Yorktown saw to it that their families observed Sabbath laws, attended weekly church services and periodic celebrations of the Eucharist, and read the Bible. Edmund Randolph credited his wife, Betsy, daughter of the devout Robert Carter Nicholas and his wife, Anne, with bringing him back to the Anglican way after several years under the influence of Enlightenment thinking absorbed during the course of his education. Not only did many women hope to live the Christian ideal in their families and communities, they also relied on their religious faith for strength as they faced the risks and pain of childbirth and the deaths of children, husbands, and friends.

Women lower down the economic scale left so few records that it is difficult to determine if they fulfilled a similar role, albeit reduced by demands of work and diminished literacy, in their families. Mrs. Ann Wager, a widow of modest means, was evidently a devout Anglican familiar with religious writings. Named mistress of the school for black children in Williamsburg, she taught from a curriculum based almost entirely on the Bible, the Anglican catechism, religious tracts, and bishops' pastoral letters, all supplied by the school's sponsors in England.

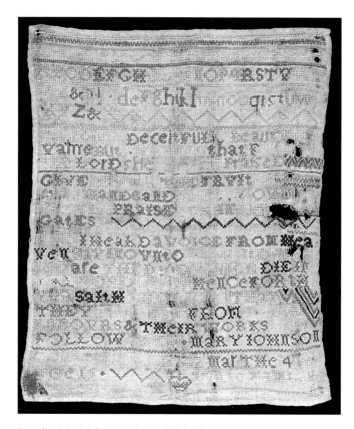

Sampler, Mary Johnson or Anne Ham[il]n, West Point, Va., 1742. A young Virginia woman worked Bible verses from Proverbs and Revelations into her sampler: "Favour is deceitful & beauty is vaine"; "let her own works praise her in the gates"; and "they may rest from their labours & their works do follow them."

THE CHURCH OF ENGLAND AND SLAVERY

Shared religious values among white and black Virginians developed slowly. Just what the spiritual lives of Africans in the colony were like, especially in the early seventeenth century, remains elusive. Whether freemen or bound laborers, they undoubtedly held onto familiar African religious practices as long as possible.

As they adapted to life in Virginia, some Africans heard about Christianity from a few sympathetic Anglicans or had contact with small groups of dissenters in the colony. The son of two blacks who arrived in 1619 was baptized in the Anglican church at Jamestown in 1624, although his parents may have been Catholic. William, son of "Negro Prosta," was baptized in York County in 1655. That same year, white planter Edmond Chisman was warned by the York County Court to keep his wife and several of his slaves away from one of the small "unlawful assemblies" of Quakers in the area. It is difficult to draw conclusions from such isolated events, but slaves somehow became familiar enough with Christianity and English ways to suppose that baptism would set them free. The General Assembly closed that loophole in 1667, but the idea still inspired slaves as late as 1730. Neither Anglicans nor dissenters taught that slavery was incompatible with Christian principles until Baptist and Methodist leaders advised converts to free their slaves in the 1760s and '70s.

Slaves had replaced white indentured servants as the principal work force in Virginia by the 1680s and '90s. Many slaveholders were indifferent to their slaves' spiritual needs; many more feared that the spiritually liberating effect of Christian teachings would make their slaves proud and unmanageable. With little support from masters or guidance from church officials in England, Anglican ministers' efforts to serve enslaved blacks were half-hearted at best.

In the 1720s, a number of priests in Virginia, among them Commissary Blair, began catechizing slaves in their parishes on the urging of the Bishop of London. Ministers William LeNeve of James City Parish, Francis Fontaine of Yorkhampton Parish, which included Yorktown, Jonathan Boucher of Caroline County, and William Willie of Sussex County all reached out to slaves. By that time, they had the cooperation of some owners who had come to feel it their duty to "Christianize" their slaves or who hoped biblical injunctions such as "servants obey your masters" would keep rebellious slaves in check.

Blair reported that sincere Christian belief distinguished a number of slaves who attended his church in Williamsburg. One may have been James Westover, who was baptized at Bruton Church as a "grown person." Several local slave owners—James Geddy, Robert Carter Nicholas, Christiana

Campbell, and Peyton Randolph—saw to it that children of their slaves were baptized. Sometimes they enrolled them in the school for black children sponsored by the Associates of Dr. Bray, a philanthropic organization in England closely tied to the Anglican church. Free black Matthew Ashby's children also attended the Bray School.

On the other hand, many slaves saw little to recommend the religion of their masters and rejected Christianity altogether. After all, many an Anglican clergymen cooperated with slave owners by counseling slaves to accept their subservient status and to obey their masters. Mrs. Wager, mistress of the Bray School, undoubtedly reinforced this message, although the schooling black children received may have had unintended consequences. Mrs. Wager taught her students rules of behavior, correct enunciation, and, most important, reading, all tools slaves could use to advantage in a society that offered them little formal protection.

List of slave baptisms, Bruton Parish Register. Courtesy, Bruton Parish Church, Williamsburg, Va.

One Tree, Many Branches

The 1707 Act of Union united Wales, Scotland, and England politically. During the remainder of the eighteenth century, Britons otherwise divided by cultural differences and historical enmities were drawn together by a shared commitment to Protestantism in the face of repeated conflict with Catholic France and Spain. Widespread suspicion of papists in Great Britain transferred to those few Catholics who settled in Virginia and the somewhat larger number in Maryland. In contrast, colonial officials generally tolerated law-abiding Protestant dissenters. Even Puritans lived peaceably in Nansemond County until 1649 when three hundred fled the colony under pressure from Governor William Berkeley, who was eager to demonstrate his loyalty to king and church during the civil war in England.

By 1700, at least twenty Quaker groups resided in Virginia despite laws that made it illegal for them to enter the colony and despite harassment from local sheriffs when they failed to attend militia musters. Huguenots arrived in Virginia in the late seventeenth and early eighteenth centuries, having first fled France for England when Louis XIV nullified the rights of French Protestants in 1685 by the Edict of Nantes. Huguenot clergymen routinely accepted Anglican ordination in England, and the laity in Virginia held onto their traditional liturgy only briefly. Eventually, they became indistinguishable from Anglicans. Virginians of Huguenot descent included the Marots and Pasteurs of Williamsburg.

An influx of Scots and Ulster Scots brought Presbyterianism to the valley of Virginia in the 1730s and '40s. Traditional Presbyterians even filled vacancies on Anglican parish vestries in some western Virginia counties. Virginia officials also accommodated smaller numbers of Moravians and other German sectaries on the frontier where Regular Baptists had been settling since the 1750s. Even the colony's capital city harbored a few non-Anglican Protestants. In 1765, a group of men gained permission from the York County Court to use a house in Williamsburg for services "according to the Practice of Protestant Dissenters of the Presbyterian denomination."

Dissenters' growing numbers notwithstanding, they labored under serious legal, financial, and social restrictions. The law required them to pay the same taxes that Anglicans did to fund ministers' salaries, construction and upkeep of Anglican churches, and poor relief. In addition, dissenters had to pay their own ministers' salaries and maintain their separate meetinghouses. Holding public office was generally off-limits to dissenters, although the House of Burgesses suffered a few Presbyterians from frontier counties to join its ranks. Sheriffs and their assistants were belligerent and occasionally violent when they broke up evangelical meetings in the 1770s. When he saw Baptist ministers preaching from their jail cells in Orange County, James Madison's inclination toward religious toleration turned into full-blown sympathy for disestablishment.

Jewish immigrants gained a foothold in Rhode Island, New York, South Carolina, and Georgia in the colonial period, but few Jews settled in Virginia until after the Revolution. Of Portuguese-Jewish descent, London-born physician John de Sequeyra immigrated to Virginia in the 1740s where he was a respected medical practitioner in Williamsburg for about fifty years. Whether Dr. de Sequeyra was willing or able to practice the Jewish faith is not known.

ENLIGHTENMENT THOUGHT

The movement known as the Enlightenment derived its name from the campaign in the seventeenth and eighteenth centuries to shine light into the recesses of the human mind benighted by superstition and ignorance. A series of scientific revelations that began during the Renaissance fostered ideas of progress and methods of reasoning that offered the first serious alternative to medieval certainties upheld by religious and civil authorities in the Christianized West. From Copernicus's theory that the earth and planets revolved around the sun to the universal laws of gravitation put forward by Isaac Newton in *Principia* (1687), the Scientific Revolution promised to liberate human beings from the fear and anxiety evoked by the unknown. Farsighted seventeenth-century philosophers such as Francis Bacon championed the modern scientific method of careful, replicable investigations and logical thinking over theological synthesis and philosophical speculation. The laws of science seemed so irrefutable and so different from the older view of nature that, by the 1690s, as one historian has put it, the "new, reforming mentality inspired a cultural war with orthodox Christianity that began in Western Europe and continued right up to the French Revolution."

It must be remembered that the outcome of this tug-of-war was not as predictable as it might first appear. Newton himself believed that the laws by which the forces of nature operated were proof of the "greater glory of God." Moreover, the Enlightenment in England and America was not so much opposed to religion as in partnership with it. Liberal clergymen in England and educated Protestant thinkers in the colonies came to see God's purpose in the ordered Newtonian universe. In other words, they could have their Bible along with their science. Other thinkers and writers caught up in the Enlightenment, particularly on the Continent, used Newton's discoveries to dispense with God altogether. In educated British and American circles, however, the "Protestant version of science" prevailed over the atheistic Enlightenment.

In Virginia, many among the educated elite came to distrust the institutional church, if not the Christian message upon which it was founded. In their view, church officials and the clergy had promulgated little more than religious superstition over the centuries, corrupting the simple teachings of Jesus for their own purposes. Many Virginia intellectuals observed that Christian churches of all denominations in their own time remained too wedded to religious truths that rested on biblical revelation alone and to accounts of miracles that withered before the "tribunal of reason." An early manifestation of this attitude is found in the case of Sir John Randolph of Williamsburg, a prominent officeholder and therefore an Anglican. Randolph noted in his will, probated in 1737, that "I have been reproached by many people especially the clergy in the article of religion" and have been called "names very familiar to blind zealots such as deist heretic and schismatic." Commissary Blair wrote the Bishop of London that Randolph "had some very wild, dissenting, and scarce Christian opinions."

Sir John's religious beliefs as explained in the will appear similar to those of prominent members of the revolutionary generation, some of whom were schooled in scientific advances and Enlightenment rationalism at the College of William and Mary. Thomas Jefferson spent several years in Williamsburg in the company of men of the Enlightenment stripe: William and Mary professor William Small, Governor Francis Fauquier, member of the Royal Society, and the scholarly George Wythe. Jefferson expressed admiration for the moral system of Jesus, which he described as the most "sublime ever preached to man," but he doubted the divinity of Christ, found the orthodox Christian doctrine of the Trinity inexplicable, and believed that God was a remote creator who had set the ordered universe in motion. This new "rational" religion had very little in common with versions of Christianity steeped in miracles and prophecy. From their study of history, philosophy, and religion, many Virginians also came to the conclusion that the human mind was created free, hence religion or matters of conscience ought to be directed only by conviction and not coerced by force of law or violence.

Personal God

By the 1750s and 1760s, evangelical Presbyterians and Separate Baptists preaching a message that emphasized the natural depravity of men and women, salvation by God's grace alone, and direct access to God for all baptized believers had made inroads in Virginia. Virginia planters who controlled the established church were suspicious of dissent and revival "enthusiasm." Out of doors or in simple meetinghouses, evangelicals' emotionally charged preaching style, which exhorted listeners to repent their sins, stood in marked contrast to the scholarly sermons Anglican clergymen read, often in monotone, from raised pulpits.

James Blair invited English Methodist George Whitefield to preach at Bruton Parish Church in 1739; Whitefield's warmly personal version of Christianity was well received. In the 1740s, Samuel Davies, a New Light Presbyterian, came to Williamsburg voluntarily on several occasions to secure the license to preach required by the General Court. As evangelical denominations grew, however, dissenters complied less willingly with these regulations.

George Whitefield, by W. Faden after a painting by John Russell, black and white engraving, England, 1768. Increasingly, Virginians after 1740 chose dissenting sects over the state-supported Church of England.

Baptists flouted licensing laws and submitted with equanimity to fines and imprisonment meted out by county officials. When sheriffs and constables disrupted Baptist meetings, they sometimes roughed up preachers and worshipers. Virginia authorities were slow to recognize that evangelicals thrived in adversity, much like the early Christians whom they tried to emulate.

"Awakened" Christians did not show customary deference when they censured high-born Anglicans for excessive drinking, gambling, and fancy dressing. Moreover, Baptists believed that each congregation was an authority unto itself, a challenge to conventional notions of church hierarchy. More alarming still, traditional class lines blurred as New Lights drew converts from all classes, even slaves.

Some leading families in Virginia were touched by the new religious "enthusiasm." The unity of the Henry family was strained when young Patrick's mother held fast to her evangelical Presbyterian faith. Councillor Robert Carter broke with the Anglican church in 1776 under the influence of the rationalism of the age as he began a spiritual journey that included conversion to the Baptist faith and later to the Church of the New Jerusalem and the teachings of Emanuel Swedenborg.

New Light Christians and Slavery

In the 1740s, evangelical Presbyterian Samuel Davies ministered to black and white congregants in Hanover County. By the 1760s and 1770s, Baptist and Methodist ministers not only preached to mixed congregations but called on their white converts to manumit their slaves. In 1771, William Lee of Greensprings in James City County expressed the dismay of many slave owners when he wrote, "The wandering new light preachers f[ro]m the Northward have put most of my Negroes crazy with their new light and their new Jerusalem." Lee's remedy: He advised his overseer to encourage all his slaves to go every Sunday to the parish church!

Blacks and whites in the Williamsburg area probably gathered together in the 1780s to hear outdoor sermons by itinerant preachers such as Baptist Joseph Mead and Methodists Joseph Pilmore and Francis Asbury. A few slaves and free blacks answered the call to preach. Local blacks may have responded to New Light Christianity in secrecy, perhaps under the influence of runaway slaves such as James Williams, James Traveller, Jack, Tom, and Harry. All were described in the *Virginia Gazette* as preachers or hymn singers, and all hid in and around Williamsburg between 1775 and 1785.

Two Williamsburg slave preachers, Moses, and, later, Gowan Pamphlet, met secretly with fellow slaves and free blacks at least as early as 1781. The group eventually allied itself with the Baptist denomination under Pamphlet's leadership to form the earliest Baptist church in America organized by and for blacks. Pamphlet organized his church for slaves and free blacks, but he

Negro Methodists holding a meeting in a Philadelphia alley, by Paul Petrovich Svinin, watercolor on paper, early nineteenth century. Courtesy, Metropolitan Museum of Art, New York, N. Y., Rogers Fund. Lingering traditional African spirituality found expression in evangelical Christianity.

soon recognized the benefits in respectability and protection that his congregation would gain if he cemented strong ties with white Baptists. Pamphlet succeeded when the white regional Dover Baptist Association approved his congregation's application for membership in 1793.

POPULAR CULTURE

Children in the eighteenth century were familiar with biblical imagery and the phraseology and rhythm of *The Book of Common Prayer* from an early age. In Anglican and dissenting homes alike, the family Bible was often the text mothers and other adults used to teach very young children the basic elements of spelling and reading. Moreover, Anglican ministers continued the traditional link between education and religious training when they opened schools for somewhat older white children. Later, they prepared young people in their teens for an oral drill on the Anglican catechism and articles of faith. Phrases such as "the patience of Job," "ashes to ashes, dust to dust," and images of the fatted calf and the prodigal son peppered the speech of people of all ranks and degrees of literacy, and turn up in the writings of educated Virginians alongside classical allusions and quotations from Greek and Roman authors.

Biblical imagery and Christian teachings were second nature to most white colonists, but they existed side by side with folk beliefs. There is evidence that folk practices, sometimes in combination with hybrid Christian beliefs, persisted in spite of the fact that traditional Protestant denominations, the rise of Enlightenment skepticism and scientific investigation, the spread of evangelical Christianity, higher literacy, and the maturation of colonial society had gradually loosened the hold of magic and superstition on the popular imagination. Almanacs published by the *Virginia Gazette*s continued to print astrological calculations and the ever-popular "anatomy," a crude human figure surrounded by the twelve signs of the zodiac that were thought to control various parts of the body. Robert Carter of Nomini Hall even renamed some of his quarters after signs of the zodiac in the late 1770s.

"Anatomy," *Virginia Almanack,* 1775. By the mid-eighteenth century, evangelical Christian teachings and advancing scientific knowledge had transformed spiritual and intellectual inquiry. Nevertheless, folk beliefs retained a hold on the popular imagination.

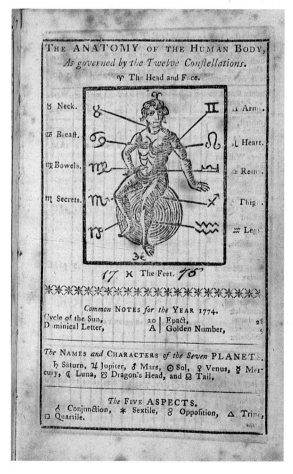

A BILL for establishing RELIGIOUS FREEDOM, printed for the consideration of the PEOPLE.

Bill for Establishing Religious Freedom, by Thomas Jefferson, 1786. Courtesy, Trustees of the Boston Public Library, Boston, Mass. As Virginians responded to the appeal of evangelical Christianity and the tolerant rationalism of the Enlightenment, they moved away from the idea of a single authoritarian church protected by the state.

LONG ROAD TO DISESTABLISHMENT

Disestablishment of the Anglican church took nearly a decade. Article sixteen of George Mason's Declaration of Rights, adopted in June 1776, stated that every person had an equal right to "free exercise" of religion, although it left the favored position of the Anglican church intact. Dissenters took the "free exercise" clause at face value, however, and began petitioning the legislature to be relieved of paying taxes for the support of the established Anglican church and to be freed from various legal restrictions. Later that year, the General Assembly agreed to suspend—but not abolish—obligatory church tax, a serious blow to an institution unaccustomed to meeting expenses though voluntary contributions. In 1779, Thomas Jefferson introduced his bill for religious freedom, but legislators in Williamsburg deemed complete disestablishment too radical at that time and tabled the measure. Dissenters' petitions kept the issue alive until it could be reconsidered after the Revolution. Meanwhile, the Assembly continued to take small steps to placate evangelicals, such as the act passed in 1780 legalizing marriages performed by dissenting ministers.

Virginia patriots were by no means of one mind about the partnership between church and state. Most shared the belief that republican government could thrive only if it were rooted in a populace with a strong moral sense, but Patrick Henry, Robert Carter Nicholas, Edmund Pendleton, and George

Mason were less sanguine than Jefferson or Madison that public and private virtue could be inculcated without the authority of an established church. In 1784, sensing that the privileged position of the Episcopal (formerly Anglican) church could not be sustained much longer, Henry and others proposed a "general assessment" that would have made all Christian churches eligible for state funds. James Madison voiced his own and most dissenters' misgivings about this proposal in his famous "Memorial and Remonstrance." He wrote that if a state could legally establish Christianity today, it could legitimately establish "any particular sect of Christians" tomorrow.

When "general assessment" failed to pass in the General Assembly (meeting in Richmond, the new capital), Madison resurrected Jefferson's old bill. With its author in France, Madison became chief advocate for its passage. The bill contained the ringing phrase, "Almighty God hath created the mind free." By acknowledging God as the source of human reason, Jefferson deftly combined religious and rationalist ideals. Both dissenters and enlightened thinkers could champion this symbol in the struggle to disassociate religion and government. Ten years after the Declaration of Rights was adopted in 1776, the efforts of New Light Christians and the Jefferson/Madison cohort gained passage of the Virginia Statute for Religious Freedom in 1786. Other states with religious establishments gradually followed, with Massachusetts the last when it disestablished the Congregational Church in 1833.

HOLLOW RING

The institution of slavery was the most obvious blemish on the accomplishments of the Revolution and religious freedom in Virginia. If passage of Jefferson's bill in 1786 ensured freedom of religion with guarantees of special privilege to none, it did so only for the white citizens of the new state. Intercultural bonds forged between white and black Baptists, Presbyterians, and Methodists in the decades before the American Revolution began to unravel by the turn of the century. Calls for evangelicals to free their slaves died out as Baptist and Methodists gained respectability and entered the mainstream of society where slavery was entrenched.

Whites had long regarded slavery and religion as a potentially dangerous combination. The mid- to late eighteenth-century revivals and awakenings only increased their anxiety. White Virginians were sure that black preachers, including Gowan Pamphlet of Williamsburg, fomented rebellion, a suspicion that appeared to be justified in 1831 when Baptist preacher Nat Turner spearheaded a revolt that took a number of lives, black and white. In the aftermath, the black Baptist meetinghouse in Williamsburg was forced to close for the better part of a year. Stricter laws soon curtailed independent African-American religious activities. Black Christians in Virginia left mixed congregations and associations after the Civil War.

Pocahontas and some other Powhatans converted to Christianity in the first two decades of white settlement in Virginia. As time went on, however, most Native Americans saw little to recommend the Christian religion in the customs of the English, which, when added to the language barrier, the strangeness of each others' lifestyles, and the dryness of the Anglican catechism, made the failure of Anglican missionary efforts inevitable. An Indian school established at Fort Christanna in the late 1710s, initially well received by Indian parents and the children they sent to be "Christianized," remained open for only a few years. Between 1700 and the Revolution, the College of William and Mary pursued the unrealistic goal of indoctrinating Indian boys sufficiently in English ways so that they could become missionaries to their people. None responded as hoped because most felt that time at William and Mary cost them valuable training in their native customs. As Native American populations dwindled and priests and traditional religions lost their power after prolonged contact with whites, remnants of several tribes withdrew to the Carolina uplands and the Ohio Country in the 1760s. There they revived their traditional cultures, including renewal of native spiritual systems. Those who remained behind in the East gradually succumbed to Christianity, especially to its evangelical strains.

Ring belonging to Mary Broadnax, Shields Tavern site, Colonial Williamsburg. The sentiment "Fear God" inside this eighteenth-century ring from Williamsburg carried over into the new republic as people continued to rely on religion to explain the joys and sorrows of everyday life.

CONCLUSION

Churches proved to be even more influential in the new republic than they had been before the Revolution precisely because they were independent of government. One historian noted, "As the Republic became democratized, it became evangelized." Ordinary people continued to rely on religion for moral direction and spiritual support as they faced the precariousness of life. Public leaders soon learned that devotion to evangelical Christianity carried political weight. In 1802, Baptists forced the sale of Episcopal (Anglican) glebe lands bought with public tax monies before 1777. When Jefferson ran for office, his enemies turned away many voters by calling his eccentric religious view atheism.

Traditionalists among postwar leaders came to view Christianity as the only force that could rescue the new nation from the social disorder that enveloped the early republic. Others were disappointed that the freedom to choose one's religious affiliation, coupled with repeated waves of revivalism in the nineteenth and twentieth centuries, did not always draw people together. Instead, it spawned denominationalism and the nonviolent but schismatic tendencies that are still characteristic of American religious life today. Americans for whom questions about abortion rights and religious displays on public property remain important issues of principle continue to involve ordinary citizens and the Supreme Court in redefining separation of church and state in the United States today.

Organized religion responded to people's changing circumstances in America. The frontier was the Promised Land to countless groups and individuals from all over the world as well as to many who struck out from the older settled areas of the colonies themselves. Methodist, Baptist, and Disciples of Christ churches sprang up throughout the American wilderness in the wake of camp meetings, week-long revivals, and circuit-riding itinerant preachers. Perhaps owing to the very freedom of worship once feared by supporters of established religion, extraordinarily large numbers of Americans today profess a belief in God and regularly attend a church, synagogue, mosque, or other formal worship service despite the ever-growing secularization of American culture in other respects.

"Freeing Religion" and the "Becoming Americans" Theme

Diverse Peoples

White English colonists brought their own religious values, customs, and assumptions to their experience in Virginia. They transplanted the state-supported Church of England to Virginia and made it the custodian of spirituality, morality, charity, and education as it was in England. The Powhatan Indians they found here believed in a distant, kindly, creator god and a pantheon of lesser deities associated with the natural world who expected to be worshiped and visited disease, crop failure, or other calamities on people who offended them. Priests possessed both curative and magical powers derived from their secret communications with the various deities. In spite of legal restrictions on non-Anglicans, Protestant dissenters began settling in Virginia in the seventeenth century. Colonial officials tolerated law-abiding Presbyterians and German sectaries on the frontier up to the middle of the eighteenth century. Black peoples, brought up in African religious systems distinguished by a close relationship between the natural world and the supernatural, the secular and the sacred, clung to familiar customs as long as they could in their forced resettlement. Under the institution of slavery, however, African religious systems did not survive intact, although individual practices persisted. Even as their traditional belief systems broke down, comparatively few slaves converted to Christianity under Anglican auspices.

Clashing Interests

People's different backgrounds, ideas, and aspirations soon came into conflict in Virginia. English settlement in Virginia embraced missionary goals as well as commercial enterprise. Most Virginia Indians resisted Christian conversion, however. They saw little in the hostility and indifference displayed by Anglican colonists to recommend the Christian religion over their own traditional beliefs. Traditional African forms of worship were largely lost to blacks after years of slavery in Virginia, although slaves did not embrace the religion of their masters in significant numbers until the religious revivals known as the Great Awakening. Many white Virginians also responded to the revivals, turning their backs on the established church to join evangelical sects. New Light Baptists and other evangelicals ignored licensing laws and demanded to be relieved of paying taxes to the established church. By that time, many intellectuals in the colony, influenced by the Enlightenment and Scientific Revolution, had begun to question the soundness of orthodox Christian ideas and the justification for an established church.

SHARED VALUES

Biblical language and imagery permeated both the oral and written cultures of all ranks of Christians. In spite of their reputations as carefree lovers of fun, Virginia gentlemen had a great interest in religion, as their libraries attest. Even those Virginians who adopted a more rational approach to religion came to that view after being reared in the Anglican church. Religious values shared by Anglicans and Protestant dissenters encouraged toleration and cooperation before mid-century. At the same time, the Anglican church and slave owners were slow to respond to the spiritual needs of bondsmen. Anglican clergymen reached out more willingly to slaves after about 1720, although they did not usually challenge the institution of slavery or refuse slave owners' requests that they preach to black congregants on the Christian virtue of obedience. Shared religious perceptions among blacks and whites were more evident in evangelical denominations after 1750. For a time, blacks and whites viewed themselves as brothers and sisters in the sight of a God who loved them all equally. Emotionally charged sermons of Baptist and other evangelical preachers appealed to worshipers from all walks of life. Over the course of the colonial period, most Native Americans shared few religious values with white Virginians whether Anglican or dissenter. Prolonged contact, on the other hand, probably did foster a limited exchange of folk knowledge among Indians, blacks, and whites.

FORMATIVE INSTITUTIONS

White Virginians, Native Americans, and African-Americans reached religious compromises through formal and informal institutions. With a commissary at its head and nearly enough ministers to fill Anglican parishes in the colony, by 1700 the Anglican establishment had become well entrenched. The real power of the church rested in the hands of local gentry vestrymen. Parish officials brought charges of bastardy, adultery, and non-attendance at church to the county courts for resolution. Church vestries taxed parishioners for support of the poor and disabled. Important "non-institutional" responsibilities fell to wives and mothers, in spite of the fact that there were no official roles for women in the Anglican church. They often taught the rudiments of reading to children in their households for which the Bible served as the textbook, and by example set the agenda for religious practices in their homes. Anglicans met with limited success in bringing Christianity to Indians and slaves in the colonial period. Young Native Americans educated at William and Mary soon returned to their traditional tribal life and religion. Slavery brought black people in Virginia to the brink of spiritual despair that was only partially alleviated by Anglican missionary efforts. Evangelical Christian sects appealed to much larger numbers of slaves.

Partial Freedoms

The institutions nurtured by a state-supported church in Virginia privileged some and disadvantaged others. Overlapping church and government institutions concentrated political power in the hands of the gentry. In turn, they imparted authority to the church. People from the upper and middle ranks of white society shared similar cultural values fostered by church attendance and socializing in the churchyard after services. These contacts likely carried over into the workaday world to give up-and-coming tradesmen and merchants a toehold in Virginia society. On the other hand, poor people got financial assistance from the church but little else. Many Anglican parishioners took great personal solace from their belief in God and felt a keen sense of Christian duty toward their fellow men. Initially, toleration of religious diversity in Virginia was not equated with freedom of religion. Consequently, dissenters could not fill public offices, nor did making their dissent official by registering with the courts according to law absolve non-Anglicans from paying public taxes to support the established church. The church in Virginia sometimes ameliorated conditions within the institution of slavery, but it also lent biblical authority to the subservient status of slaves. Church attendance by slaves and servants depended upon their masters' will. The Anglican church did not countenance rituals or beliefs of Native Americans, but a sustained missionary effort among Virginia Indians was barely perceptible. For their part, few Indians warmed to the Christian religion in the colonial period.

Revolutionary Promise

In Virginia, persistent injustices, inequalities, and unbalanced power relationships contained seeds of future religious discord. Isolated incidents of religious persecution before 1700 gave way to relatively peaceful coexistence among religious groups before the middle of the eighteenth century. Thereafter, the struggle to gain religious freedom went hand in hand with political events that transformed Virginia from colony to state, although disestablishment of the Protestant Episcopal Church (formerly the Church of England) was not achieved until ten years after political independence was declared. In 1786, the unlikely partnership between dissenters and Enlightenment thinkers freed Virginians to worship, or not, as their consciences dictated. Religious freedom had a hollow ring for slaves, who prayed under the watchful eyes of their masters. Moreover, contact with outside cultures eventually undermined Native American belief systems.

CONNECTIONS TO OTHER "BECOMING AMERICANS" STORY LINES

TAKING POSSESSION

As colonists took up land in Virginia, Anglican parishes regularly processioned the bounds to confirm titles to it. Anglican parishes owned farms or plantations known as glebe lands that ministers could work themselves for profit or rent out to supplement their salaries, which were set by law. After disestablishment, there was a clamor to have these lands, purchased with tax monies in the colonial period, removed from church ownership and sold to benefit the public. Land-hungry colonists and British officials concluded that encroachment on Indian lands and the near-extermination of native populations were justified in part because most Native Americans did not embrace the monotheistic religion and other customs of the invaders.

ENSLAVING VIRGINIA

The Anglican church in Virginia tolerated slavery. The Associates of Dr. Bray, a missionary organization in England, was especially concerned with slaves but focused only on saving their souls and improving their treatment, not on the abolition of slavery. Some masters feared that the spiritually liberating effect of Christianity would foster rebelliousness in their bondsmen. Individual ministers and owners had slaves instructed in the Anglican catechism. They often stressed humility and obedience as the most desirable Christian values. Neither the Anglican church nor the law recognized slave marriages, but ministers (with permission from a broad cross section of local masters) baptized nearly one thousand slaves, most of them infants, at Bruton Parish Church. Mrs. Wager, tutor at the Bray School for black children in Williamsburg, doubtless shared some of the same goals and assumptions as owners and ministers, but she also taught slaves to read, a skill that could be used to advantage by those eager to circumvent controls forced on them by white society. Many more slaves were drawn to the Baptists and other New Light evangelical sects than had responded to Christianity through the established church. The evangelical Christian message of equality before God merged in African-American culture with Old Testament images of deliverance to give many slaves a stronger spiritual identity and new inner resources with which to resist the effects of slavery.

REDEFINING FAMILY

Belief in a father God who guided and cared for the human beings he created was reflected in the patriarchal arrangement in eighteenth-century white families. Husbands headed households, and family values were based on religious values. Wives often exerted important influence on religious practices in their families, even though they were subordinate to their husbands. Anglican sermons and the seating arrangements in some churches reinforced notions of patriarchal family structure. Ann Wager and Anne Nicholas, Williamsburg women of different social ranks, represented the ideal of Anglican womanhood as models of piety for their friends and relations and initiators of religious faith in the children they taught. Virginians often kept birth and death dates in family Bibles, although vestries officially recorded these events. The established church did not recognize slave marriages, while marriages of free persons had its blessing and protection, and vestries provided support for free families fallen on hard times. White family structure came under some pressure as evangelical sects won more converts. It was often a woman who responded to religious revivals, which disrupted family unity if her husband was loyal to the Anglican church as was the case with Patrick Henry's parents.

BUYING RESPECTABILITY

Clergymen of all stripes, playwrights, and lawmakers had long warned that the spread of luxury in England would spawn "dangerous insubordination in society" as people sought to buy their way up the social ladder. Pulpits—Anglican and dissenter alike—and newspapers in America rang with similar admonitions about the disturbing growth of luxury and extravagance. As one writer put it in the *Virginia Gazette,* "Luxury poisons a whole Nation and all Conditions and Ranks of Men are Confounded." Baptists and other New Light Christians denounced the lifestyles of the well-to-do, decrying their devotion to fancy dress and games of chance. Evangelicals argued that the gentry's self-serving habits reflected a shallow faith. The new consumerism became apparent in Anglican churches in eighteenth-century Virginia. A new church for Bruton Parish completed in 1715 came into being in part because the burgesses, governor, and Council wanted to worship in an appropriately appointed state church. The church included a fine box for the governor and eventually a steeple and organ. Private pews and burial inside the church or beneath elaborate stones in the churchyard bestowed prestige on those who could afford them. Weekly Anglican church services made for convenient display of fine coaches and clothing. Mrs. Anne Nicholas's piety did not stop her from ordering an expensive prayer book from England.

CHOOSING REVOLUTION

In the 1750s and '60s, evangelical Presbyterians and Baptists became less and less willing to be constrained by rules that advantaged the Church of England in the colony. They precipitated a struggle for religious freedom that challenged the centralized church establishment even before the Stamp Act crisis gave evidence that changes were underway in the political arena. In the twenty-five years before events in 1776 forced Virginians to choose between rebellion and loyalty to the king, the sermons of George Whitefield, Samuel Davies, and others during the series of religious revivals we know as the Great Awakening had already inspired many colonists to make decisions that upset the status quo. When they turned their backs on the Anglican establishment, evangelical dissenters not only challenged civil authority, but questioned its legal partnership with a particular church. Moreover, traditional class lines blurred as black and white, rich and poor, and free and slave worshipers mingled at gatherings where they heard about a God who loved them all equally.

In the political arena, Baptists and Presbyterians driven by evangelical fervor to practice their religion unmolested, and men such as Thomas Jefferson and James Madison, who believed the human mind was created free, persuaded the General Assembly to pass a law in 1786 guaranteeing free exercise of religion. Before the Revolution, his distaste for church establishments notwithstanding, Jefferson had helped "cook up" the fast day observed on June 1, 1774, at Bruton Parish and other Anglican churches to show solidarity with the citizens of Boston. Some ministers praised the Revolution from the pulpit as God's vehicle for bringing the people in America into the Promised Land. On the other hand, ministers loyal to the Crown continued to stress that the king remained God's principal representative on earth, who carried out his duty with the help of a select group of high-ranking individuals. Meanwhile, George Washington and other military leaders recognized the importance of religious counsel for their troops. Many Episcopal (formerly Anglican) clergymen who supported independence became chaplains, and several dissenting ministers successfully petitioned the Assembly to be permitted to do the same.

Story Line Team: John Turner, Janet Guthrie, Linda Hamric, Mary Jamerson, Emily James, B. J. Pryor, Linda Rowe, Heather Slining, Laurie Suber, Bill Weldon, and Terry Yemm.

FURTHER READING

Bond, Edward L. *Damned Souls in a Tobacco Colony: Religion in Seventeenth-Century Virginia.* Macon, Ga.: Mercer University Press, 2000.

———. "Source of Knowledge, Source of Power: The Supernatural World of English Virginia, 1607–1624." *Virginia Magazine of History and Biography,* CVII (2000), pp. 105–138.

Bonomi, Patricia U. *Under the Cope of Heaven: Religion, Society, and Politics in Colonial America.* New York: Oxford University Press, 1986.

Butler, Jon. *Awash in a Sea of Faith: Christianizing the American People.* Cambridge, Mass.: Harvard University Press, 1990.

Fray, Silvia R., and Betty Wood. *Come Shouting to Zion: African-American Protestantism in the American South and British Caribbean to 1830.* Chapel Hill, N. C.: University of North Carolina Press, 1998.

Gaustad, Edwin S. *Faith of Our Fathers: Religion and the New Nation.* San Francisco: Harper & Row, 1987. Rev. ed., *Neither King nor Prelate: Religion and the New Nation, 1776–1826.* Grand Rapids, Mich.: Eerdmans, 1993.

———. *Sworn on the Altar of God: A Religious Biography of Thomas Jefferson.* Grand Rapids, Mich.: William B. Eerdmans Publishing Co., 1996.

Gunderson, Joan R. "The Non-Institutional Church: The Religious Role of Women in Eighteenth-Century Virginia." *Historical Magazine of the Protestant Episcopal Church,* LI (1982), pp. 347–357.

———. "The Search for Good Men: Recruiting Ministers in Colonial Virginia." *Ibid.,* XLVIII (1979), pp. 453–464.

Hall, Timothy D. *Contested Boundaries: Itinerancy and the Reshaping of the Colonial American Religious World.* Durham, N. C.: Duke University Press, 1994.

Holmes, David L. *A Brief History of the Episcopal Church.* Valley Forge, Pa.: Trinity Press International, 1993.

Ingersoll, Thomas N. "'Release us out of this Cruell Bondegg': An Appeal from Virginia in 1723." *William and Mary Quarterly,* 3rd Ser., LI (1994), pp. 777–782.

Isaac, Rhys. *The Transformation of Virginia, 1740–1790.* Chapel Hill, N. C.: University of North Carolina Press, 1982.

Mathews, Donald G. *Religion in the Old South.* Chicago: University of Chicago Press, 1977.

Mbiti, John S. *African Religions and Philosophy.* Portsmouth, N. H.: Heinemann, 1990.

Nelson, John K. *A Blessed Company: Parishes, Parsons, and Parishioners in Anglican Virginia, 1690–1776.* Chapel Hill, N. C.: University of North Carolina Press, 2002.

Peterson, Merrill D., and Robert C. Vaughan, eds. *Virginia Statute for Religious Freedom: Its Evolution and Consequences in American History.* Cambridge: Cambridge University Press, 1988.

Raboteau, Albert J. *Slave Religion: "The Invisible Institution" in the Antebellum South.* New York: Oxford University Press, 1978.

Rountree, Helen C. *Powhatan Indians of Virginia: Their Traditional Culture.* Norman, Okla.: University of Oklahoma Press, 1989.

Sobel, Mechal. *Trabelin' On: The Slave Journey to an Afro-Baptist Faith.* Princeton, N. J.: Princeton University Press, 1988.

Thomson, Robert Polk. "The Reform of the College of William and Mary, 1763–1780." American Philosophical Society, *Proceedings,* CXV (1971), pp. 187–213.

Upton, Dell. *Holy Things and Profane: Anglican Parish Churches in Colonial Virginia.* Cambridge, Mass: MIT Press, 1986; and review by Joan R. Gundersen, *William and Mary Quarterly,* XLVI (1989), pp. 379–382.

Wood, Gordon S. "Enlightenment" and "The Celebration of Commerce" in *The Radicalism of the American Revolution.* New York: Alfred A. Knopf, 1992.

Woodson, Carter G. *The History of the Negro Church.* Washington, D. C.: Associated Publishers, 1992.

APPENDIX A
AN INTERPRETIVE FRAMEWORK

We offer readers who know their Virginia history the following demonstration that the narrative structure proposed in this plan can give museum interpreters and visiting classroom teachers all the scope, drama, and color they need to describe the settlement of the Chesapeake region and the growth and development of England's largest and wealthiest mainland American colony. The headings correspond to those outlined on pages 12–13.

DIVERSE PEOPLES

The encounter of immigrants and indigenous peoples in the New World setting of Virginia was a dynamic process. It involved a cast of characters that changed across time and space. The earliest English immigrants were a mixed bunch despite their common national background. A few came from the ruling ranks of England's landed and commercial classes. The majority were farmers—yeomen and husbandmen—or laborers.

The colonists encountered native peoples in Virginia. Chesapeake Algonquians recognized many village cultures, all of which were organized around an understanding of social order, justice, and authority that varied profoundly from English norms. The contest between the Indians and the invading Europeans grew increasingly unequal as the seventeenth century wore on. English newcomers enjoyed decisive advantages, including their superior numbers, greater firepower, immunity to the diseases they spread among the native peoples, and an unshakable belief in their own cultural superiority. Before the end of the century, Englishmen managed to confine Indian peoples to reservations or push them to the frontiers of European settlement.

As the number of Indians declined, they were replaced by a growing number of enslaved Africans. Virginians forcibly imported Africans by the tens of thousands from many parts of West Africa. Significant numbers came from the West Indies as well. The trade in unfree African labor continued well into the eighteenth century.

Large numbers of working-class people from English towns and cities migrated to Virginia in the eighteenth century. By mid-century, other Europeans, principally Scots, Ulster Scots, and German-speaking settlers, began filling up the backcountry of Virginia. Unlike earlier colonists, these newcomers encountered a native-born, or creole, population of whites and blacks that was already several generations old.

CLASHING INTERESTS

The multiplicity of cultural groups in Virginia confounded and sometimes overwhelmed Old World beliefs and practices. Furthermore, the unfamiliar conditions immigrants encountered in their new home caused many newcomers to question their traditional beliefs, including, ultimately, the rules and assumptions that ordered society. For example, the Virginia climate and terrain hastened the acceptance of slash-and-burn agriculture as English farmers learned to become successful tobacco planters. In turn, market-driven, capitalistic agriculture altered traditional attitudes about property ownership, economic advantage, social control, education, salvation, and family.

The population of the colony became thoroughly biracial and, to a lesser degree, multi-ethnic by the time of the Revolution. Some vestiges of European and African institutions and values could still be recognized, but the nature of Virginia society had become profoundly different by the close of the colonial period. The crisis of the Revolution revealed the extent of those differences. Virginians discovered that they were no longer Englishmen, Africans, Germans, or Scotsmen living abroad. They had become fully developed, indigenous, American-Virginian peoples.

SHARED VALUES

Forging this new social and political reality was not simple or easy. Different peoples held different convictions about the nature of a "right and proper" society. Conflicts were easily provoked, given the disposition of Anglo-Virginians to subordinate other cultures and races. Europeans often came to blows with Native Americans over the profoundly different meaning each group gave to the idea of private property. Frequent violence linked the destiny of these two peoples, however one-sided the contest.

Collisions among other immigrant groups produced accommodations that gradually came to be perceived as virtues in themselves. Despite English determination to set society's standards and make its governing rules, other ethnic Europeans went to considerable pains to preserve their separate cultural identities. African-Americans, too, struggled desperately to create a sustainable hybrid culture in the face of slavery. Thus, all these groups, each in its own way, made claims to self-determination. That aspiration ultimately found fulfillment in the notion of individual freedom of choice.

Free whites shared other expectations for the good life in Virginia. Whether they had been pushed out of the Rhineland by poverty and persecution or pulled up stakes in lowland Virginia in the quest for cheap land in the backcountry, free settlers were eager to capitalize on the colony's seemingly inexhaustible resources. The abundance of land encouraged the widespread belief that enterprise and hard work would bring economic sufficiency and a higher standard of living for one's self or one's children. The colony's resources were irresistible temptations to speculators, monopolizers, and wheeler-dealers. Rapaciousness and greed added aggressive energy to the pursuit of plenty.

The division of spoils among individuals and groups with competing interests contributed to people's feeling that they had a stake in the new land, however unequally. Virginia was still a face-to-face society in the eighteenth century. People knew each other by reputation and lineage, if not personally. These familiar and meaningful associations were strengthened by a system of patronage. A network of binding ties created a powerful local identification and a loyalty to place, whether that place was a quarter, plantation, neighborhood, or town. A fierce sense of localism mitigated somewhat the rugged individualism of many Virginians.

FORMATIVE INSTITUTIONS

Over time, local and provincial institutions blunted the differences that divided people who held competing interests and contested values. Virginians developed a habit—some said a talent—for a kind of improvised pragmatism that helped them patch over the contradictions in society. For example, rural neighborhoods became the arenas where new rules for local leadership were worked out. Because the Virginia frontier was settled primarily by residents from older regions, most newly settled neighborhoods experienced a high turnover of people moving in and moving out. Despite the rapid replacement of the population, neighborhoods themselves played a central role in freeholders' lives because political authority was vested in local offices, regardless of who filled them. Traditional English concepts of inherited local leadership counted for very little in the fluid communities of Virginia. Necessity required that economically successful planters, whatever their background, be granted authority over their neighbors.

Public institutions of church and state arbitrated conflicts in settled parts of the colony, often with unanticipated consequences. Virginians in the seventeenth century quickly established English-style county courts, for instance, in hopes that these age-old local institutions would extend their traditional protections to elite property owners. Unexpectedly, Virginia courts became equally accessible to men of lesser status who could afford to buy inexpensive land that would have been beyond their reach in England. It followed that local courts regulated an extraordinarily wide range of economic interests in Virginia. Courts thus helped to channel and validate the disciplined pursuit of individual self-interest.

The church played an important mediating role too. Anglican clergymen abetted their white parishioners by preaching to slaves about the virtue of obedience. The Book of Common Prayer enjoined bondsmen to accept their masters' authority. On the other hand, New Light Presbyterian and Baptists churches emphasized personal piety and public morality. They gave dissenters an independent voice in opposition to the established church presided over by the gentry.

The Virginia General Assembly developed into a highly valued institution where private interests and their public consequences were debated and legislated. After 1765, when many Virginians began to fear that British nullification of American-made laws threatened the existence of their colonial legislature, the colony's leaders deliberately cast the elected assembly in the role of public protector and spokesman for the "people's" interests. The notion of the House of Burgesses as a broadly representative body elevated the ideal of self-government into one of the defining principles that gave meaning to being an American.

PARTIAL FREEDOMS

Stubborn tradition and persistent inequalities of wealth and privilege left the promise of the Revolution unfulfilled for many. In principle, the concepts of liberty and equality applied to all. In practice, only property-holding white males enjoyed full citizenship. Privilege was deeply rooted. Local political systems were a major obstacle to more democratic participation in the civic enterprise. Local politics remained highly oligarchic. County commissioners were appointed, not elected. They exercised wide discretionary powers, from setting tax rates to naming minor public officials. Furthermore, they were self-perpetuating. So were Anglican vestries and urban hustings courts. These tenacious local oligarchies, coupled with the infrequent election of burgesses, excluded poor and middling Virginians from most opportunities to participate in governing their communities. Although they were called into question, even before the Revolution, traditional notions of social hierarchy and deference remained entrenched. They blinded Virginians to the true meaning of equality. Racial prejudice reinforced and perpetuated these patriarchal attitudes as long as planters and their poorer neighbors deemed them necessary to control the enslaved labor force.

Ironically, other obstacles to full achievement of liberty and equality were embedded in the ideology of the Revolution itself. The racism buried in the revolutionary rhetoric of the Virginia constitution was one. The authors' language camouflaged the social and economic differences between rich and poor whites by giving them all a common racial heritage. The stain of racial prejudice on the tenets of democratic republicanism became an eradicable blemish on political philosophy in Virginia. It condemned African-Americans to the status of perpetual outcasts.

The social realities experienced by all the mainland colonies were sufficiently similar so that most colonists could make a common cause of the issues they understood to be at stake in the struggle with Great Britain. A sense of destiny directed Virginians' attention to events beyond their borders. The *Virginia Gazettes* frequently reported British attacks on colonies to the north, and Virginia leaders were in regular correspondence with compatriots in Philadelphia, Boston, and other trouble spots. News of Great Britain's intimidation of the New York General Assembly and its punitive response to the Boston "tea party" spurred Virginians into action. This unity of purpose and the knowledge that people in Massachusetts, New York, and other colonies would stand shoulder-to-shoulder with them emboldened rebels in Virginia as separation from Britain became their only choice. The colonies' ultimate victory validated the revolutionaries' ideals and strengthened their sense of American identity.

REVOLUTIONARY PROMISE

The most positive and progressive American ideals have always exerted a powerful hold on the imaginations of those to whom they have been denied. The unenfranchised were legion at the end of the colonial period. The conservative interpretation of the revolutionary philosophy in Virginia proved unfriendly to those seeking to extend the limits of eighteenth-century ownership.

The ruling classes could not completely shut down the reform impulse. Some Virginians were already growing uncomfortable with slavery. More and more of them began to challenge it, however indirectly. For a brief period in the 1780s and 1790s, they were able to ease restrictions on manumissions. The reformers' zeal eventually met a stronger force. White Virginians feared the growing numbers of free blacks. Their anxieties ran too deep for abolitionists to overcome. Faced with whites' determined opposition to their freedom, many African-Americans took matters into their own hands and ran away to the free states in the North.

Extending the franchise to poorer whites involved another hard-fought struggle, this one successful. Non-freeholders demanded the vote almost from the moment the Constitution of 1776 was adopted. Notwithstanding, the powerful Jeffersonian idea that only independent yeoman farmers could resist the corrupting influence of special interests remained the keystone of agrarian republicanism in Virginia for decades. Its logic defeated all early efforts at electoral reform. The vote was finally extended to male leaseholders and householders in 1829. Universal manhood suffrage was not accepted in the state until 1850. Women did not enter the voting booth until 1920 when a majority of other states ratified the Nineteenth Amendment.

APPENDIX B
WILLIAMSBURG RESTORED

In addition to the story lines that tell the "Becoming Americans" story, another topic—the ongoing work of restoration and the never-ending research that continually revises our understanding and interpretation of the eighteenth century—deserves attention. It has fascinated visitors for over seventy years. Visitors frequently ask how the town looked before John D. Rockefeller, Jr., began the restoration. Half a century later, they are surprised to find that our historians, archaeologists, curators, conservators, and architectural historians are still searching for answers to historical problems that remain unsolved. "You haven't finished studying the town?" they often inquire. The answer, of course, is that there is no end to historical research. Each generation draws its own perspective on the past and restates the questions it thinks are most important.

The process of discovery holds great interest for many visitors. Their curiosity for a glimpse behind the scenes and their eagerness to learn how scholars uncover secrets of the eighteenth century give interpreters an excellent opportunity to demonstrate that history is a creative endeavor. Many visitors are surprised to learn that studying history is not cut and dried or that historical facts don't speak for themselves. Giving visitors a chance to watch us work will help many of them understand that history writing has its own history.

The history of the restoration, now more than seventy years old, leaves no doubt that Colonial Williamsburg is also a museum of a museum, however much it is primarily a museum of eighteenth-century history. Our historians and preservationists frequently remind us that restored Williamsburg—its buildings, its "interior decoration," and its gardens—have exerted a potent influence on the look and landscape of twentieth-century America. As the century draws to a close, there is growing appreciation for Colonial Williamsburg's leadership in the Colonial Revival movement. Already some policy decisions have been made that have resulted in identifying and preserving the most significant features of restored and reconstructed Williamsburg. Williamsburg's role as a powerful tastemaker in modern America is an element of the preservation story that deserves wider telling.

The history of the restoration has been told before, mainly by our architects, archaeologists, and, to a certain extent, tradespeople. Craft demonstrations, the Bassett Hall exhibits on the Rockefeller family, and numerous popular publications have described how specialists on our staff re-create the appearance of times past. These people are skillful scene setters. We know—but visitors need to know too—that interpreters help fill in those re-created scenes with the historical figures, activities, ideas, and events that provide the comprehensive interpretation of the past that visitors encounter in the Historic Area. We should therefore always be looking for occasions to interpret the ever-popular story of the restoration of Williamsburg, telling the many ways we practice the craft of history to bring an eighteenth-century town and a busy community back to life.